What Your Colleagues Are Saying . . .

"How many times have we told kids to listen to each other and treat each other kindly? How often do we lament at year's end, 'Maybe next year I'll get a group who can work together?' Collaboration and cooperation do not emerge magically. We must explicitly teach kids the social strategies of collaborative behavior, to listen attentively, ask follow-up questions, and disagree agreeably. This resource, *Teaching the Social Skills of Academic Interaction*, does exactly that. Through a series of engaging slides, lessons, and activities, kids learn and practice important SEL strategies that will lead to more learning, greater achievement, and an inviting and fun classroom environment where kids work collaboratively and independently and develop a sense of agency. Smokey and Nancy understand that this is really about going slow to go fast. When we take time to explicitly model and teach kids how to interact and work together and then give them time to practice, much of the rest falls into place. It is way past due time for this resource. Teachers need it and will love it, but more importantly, so will kids!"

—STEPHANIE HARVEY, Co-author of *The Comprehension Toolkit*

"*Teaching the Social Skills of Academic Interaction* recognizes the importance of establishing an emotionally healthy classroom—a classroom where students have been taught to manage their emotions, to build relationships, and to work effectively with one another. The easy-to-use lessons in this book connect with students by giving them more responsibility, more control, and more choice. As Daniels and Steineke say, the best classrooms are those in which students are treated like the people they want to become. This book helps teachers to build those classrooms. I highly recommend it."

—KELLY GALLAGHER, Author of *Write Like This*

"Harvey 'Smokey' Daniels and Nancy Steineke write with humor and common sense about the challenges of bringing a diversity of students into harmony each school year. . . . This book holds the research and the tools to change the way classrooms operate. With 35 lessons (one for each week of school) and the systematic guidance of thoughtful, smart colleagues to explain the importance and likely obstacles to each lesson, teachers will learn to guide student groups in productive, dynamic ways."

—PENNY KITTLE, Author of *Book Love*

"Do you cringe when it's time for small-group work? Do you find that work time gets too unruly when students have a chance to discuss with partners? If so, you need this book. Smokey and Nancy, the king and queen of conversation, guide teachers in setting up systems and structures that allow for purposeful talk to happen in the classroom. Teachers pondering how to prepare students for the CCSS speaking and listening standards and, more importantly, as effective communicators for the world outside of school, will truly appreciate all this book has to offer."

—CRIS TOVANI, Author of *So What Do They Really Know?*

"Group work no longer begins and ends in the classroom. It's a reality—a life skill. My favorite part about the book is that it works with whatever content you're teaching. The lessons are focused on the students' interactions while the content of the work is reflective of what is happening in the classroom, so it's not 'another' thing to do on your already long list of things to teach. Clever and creative, this is a valuable resource for teachers of all disciplines."

—AIMEE BUCKNER, Author of *Notebook Know-How*

TEACHING THE SOCIAL SKILLS OF ACADEMIC INTERACTION

Dedicated to David Johnson, Roger Johnson, and Edythe Johnson Holubec.
We are forever indebted to your groundbreaking
research in the field of cooperation and group dynamics.

HARVEY "SMOKEY" DANIELS • NANCY STEINEKE

TEACHING THE SOCIAL SKILLS OF ACADEMIC INTERACTION

Step-by-Step Lessons for
Respect, **Responsibility**, and **Results**

35 Projectable Lessons!

Grades 4–12

With Illustrations by
SATYA MOSES

CL CORWIN LITERACY

CORWIN
A SAGE Company

FOR INFORMATION:

Corwin
A SAGE Company
2455 Teller Road
Thousand Oaks, California 91320
(800) 233-9936
www.corwin.com

SAGE Publications Ltd.
1 Oliver's Yard
55 City Road
London EC1Y 1SP
United Kingdom

SAGE Publications India Pvt. Ltd.
B 1/I 1 Mohan Cooperative Industrial Area
Mathura Road, New Delhi 110 044
India

SAGE Publications Asia-Pacific Pte. Ltd.
3 Church Street
#10-04 Samsung Hub
Singapore 049483

Publisher: Lisa Luedeke
Editorial Development Manager: Julie Nemer
Editorial Assistants: Francesca Dutra Africano and Emeli Warren
Production Editor: Melanie Birdsall
Copy Editor: Talia Greenberg
Typesetter: C&M Digitals (P) Ltd.
Proofreader: Laura Webb
Indexer: Judy Hunt
Cover and Interior Designer: Gail Buschman
Marketing Manager: Maura Sullivan

Illustrations by Satya Moses.

Clipart used with permission of www.clipart.com.

Common Core State Standards (CCSS) cited throughout the book are copyright © 2010 National Governors Association Center for Best Practices and Council of Chief State School Officers. All rights reserved.

Printed in the United States of America

Library of Congress Cataloging-in-Publication Data

Daniels, Harvey

Teaching the social skills of academic interaction, grades 4-12 : step-by-step lessons for respect, responsibility, and results/Harvey "Smokey" Daniels, Nancy Steineke.

pages cm
Includes bibliographical references and index.

ISBN 978-1-4833-5095-0

1. Social skills—Study and teaching (Elementary)—Activity programs. 2. Social skills—Study and teaching (Secondary)—Activity programs. I. Steineke, Nancy

HQ783.D2883 2014
302′.14071—dc23   2014015502

This book is printed on acid-free paper.

14 15 16 17 18 10 9 8 7 6 5 4 3 2 1

Contents

Part II. Lessons for Building Social-Academic Skills

Visit the companion website at
www.corwin.com/teachingsocialskills
for lesson slides and other downloadable resources.

Acknowledgments

The two of us have been co-authoring books for quite a while; in fact, this is our seventh collaboration. So, to begin with, we'd like to give each other a big fist bump (see page 48). Since this is a book about collaboration, it would be pretty embarrassing if the two of us didn't get along. But it just gets easier. We really show each other Friendliness and Support (see the next 230 pages), and it works.

Our spouses, Elaine and Bill, have been virtual co-authors with us over the past fifteen years. Thanks to them, we enjoy Home Court Advantage every day (see page 49). They are our first readers, mildest critics, and favorite travel partners. As we've conducted multiday institutes around the country (fifty-three so far, but who's counting?) the four of us have shared delightful conversations and delectable dinners in almost every state. Idaho, here we come!

When we brought this somewhat unusual project to Corwin, they immediately got it. Our editor and old friend Lisa Luedeke guided us through every step with steady and much-appreciated enthusiasm. Julie Nemer, Melanie Birdsall, and designer Gail Buschman gave us an awesome cover, a catchy interior, and a painless production process. Francesca Dutra Africano and Emeli Warren provided patient and unfailing support, early and late. Maura Sullivan, marketer extraordinaire, now takes over to help the book find its hopefully vast audience. And it has been great to know that Director of Editorial and Professional Learning Lisa Shaw and President Mike Soules have taken a personal interest in this project.

The beautiful illustrations in the book, and the eight adorable students you will soon meet, are the work of Satya Moses, an artist from Dublin, New Hampshire. Every Saturday morning for four months, the three of us got on the phone and worked through Satya's sketches, then drawings, and then colored finals for literally hundreds of slides. We think the results are amazing, and they reflect our attitude toward kids: they want to work hard, do well, and have fun. Now that you've bought the book and admired the drawings, we can reveal that Satya was only nineteen years old when he made them. He is now off to art school. Stand by for the sequel, Satya!

This book marks a transition for Nancy. After several decades as a teacher in suburban Chicago (shout out to all her former students from Andrew High School!), she will be writing, speaking, and consulting full-time in districts around the country by the time you read this. Smokey will continue sallying forth from Santa Fe into the same realms; we hope to share a stage as often as possible.

Every idea in every one of our books traces back to kids, to the thousands of students we've been lucky to hang out and learn with over our fortunate years in this profession. Thanks, you guys, every one. Even Daniel and Devin. *Especially* Daniel and Devin.

Readers, we hope you enjoy this book, and that it helps you get closer to your kids. In these hard teaching times, our only hope is to redouble our commitment to the precious beings we work with every day.

Friendship and support—first, foremost, and always.

Publisher's Acknowledgments

Corwin gratefully acknowledges the contributions of the following reviewers:

Sara Ahmed
Educator, Middle School History
The Bishop's School
La Jolla, CA

Cindy Gagliardi
English Teacher
Chatham High School
Chatham, NJ

Kym Sheehan
Curriculum and Instruction Specialist
Charlotte County Public Schools
Port Charlotte, FL

Jennifer Wheat Townsend
Literacy Specialist
MSD Pike Township
Indianapolis, IN

Part I

Social-Academic Skills: The Missing Link

Chapter 1

The Problem and the Opportunity

Social-Emotional Learning and Academic Engagement

Would you like your students to *behave?* By which we mean:

- Be kind and supportive toward one another?
- Work productively with partners and in teams?
- Sustain lively and thoughtful discussions in small groups?
- Maintain focus and productivity?
- Help each other dig deep into curricular topics?
- Show classmates respect, not aggression and put-downs?
- Create a classroom climate of curiosity, focus, and fun?
- Get good test scores *and* be good human beings?

Us, too. Creating supportive classroom communities has been a subtext of seven books we have previously written together. Here, we bring it to the foreground.

Wherever we work in schools (twenty-three states last year) the number one question teachers ask is: "How can I get these kids to work together?" Sometimes, they say this with emphasis on the word *these,* accompanied by a subtle eye-roll, as in, "You have no idea what I am up against here."

No matter how politely we phrase it, a perennial problem is that our kids don't all get along. They don't work together easily. Too often, they hassle, disrespect, and put each other down. When we place them with partners or in groups, they goof off, waste time, careen off task, or pick on each other. We watch this with rising levels of discomfort, trying to put a lid on the fractiousness, the negativity. After a while, we may feel compelled to abandon our dream of an interactive classroom, push the desks back into rows, and hand out some worksheets, just to calm the kids down. If we get frustrated enough, we'll cast blame upon last year's teachers, or the kids' parents, or their neighborhood. "Maybe next year," we think to ourselves, "I'll get a class that can collaborate."

Wherever we work in schools, the number one question teachers ask is: "How can I get these kids to work together?"

No one is born knowing how to be a responsible team member. These skills have to be learned . . . we have to *teach* this stuff!

But *no one* is born knowing how to be a good friend, a supportive partner, or a responsible team member. These skills have to be learned. Or, to put it another way, we have to *teach* this stuff! It's not fair for us to complain about chaos or low morale in our classrooms before we even try to fix it.

Now, we are not completely denying the reality of what we teachers call "good groups" and "bad groups." Sometimes, the district computer sends us a real doozy of a class list. You start to wonder, are they punishing me for something? But mostly, good groups—classes of kids who work well together—are made, not born. That's one thing that this book is about: taking command of the interactions in our classroom, not being victims of the luck of the draw.

What's Been Missing in School Reform

After decades of academic-based reforms like No Child Left Behind and Race to the Top, school people are realizing that we have indeed left something crucial behind. The vital social skills of successful academic work are being neglected in today's classrooms, despite their centrality in college and career readiness. Kids are living in (and leaving) schools without acquiring the habits of effective collaboration with others. They aren't learning how to be respectful, friendly, cooperative, and empathic. They aren't growing as responsible team members, supportive partners, and reliable workers. They aren't practicing the social skills that lead to success in school, college, or anywhere else they might wind up.

Some call this overlooked domain "emotional intelligence," or "soft skills," or "interpersonal skills," or "positive behavior," or even "twenty-first century skills." Under these various banners, school districts across the country have belatedly begun addressing the issues of student emotional states, school climate, "positive behavior interventions and supports," social skills, and collaboration. A stunningly diverse (and otherwise polarized) assortment of school people and vendors are jumping aboard.

It seems fair to say that we are enjoying a boom in "social-emotional learning," commonly shorthanded to SEL. This diffuse movement encompasses a wide range of both commercial and nonprofit programs that teach kids how to manage their emotions, build relationships, and work effectively, both as individuals and as teammates. Early research on these models has been very promising: a major meta-analysis of 213 studies showed an average 11 percent gain in academic performance for kids receiving such instruction (Durlak et al., 2011).

Why We Must Teach Social-Academic Skills Now

A variety of factors has emerged to drive the awareness of SEL, to raise our sense of urgency, and to fuel its implementation in today's schools.

The Common Core State Standards Requirements

The CCSS standards for Speaking and Listening (2010) explicitly call for all students to develop the social skills of academic interaction. The anchor standards require students to collaborate effectively "in pairs, small group and large group discussions" from kindergarten through high school. Grade-level standards get more precise and challenging as kids move up. In kindergarten, the CCSS expects children to:

- Participate in collaborative conversations with diverse partners about *kindergarten topics and texts* with peers and adults in small and larger groups
- Follow agreed-upon rules for discussions (e.g., listening to others and taking turns speaking about the topics and texts under discussion)
- Continue a conversation through multiple exchanges
- Confirm understanding of a text read aloud or information presented orally or through other media by asking and answering questions about key details and requesting clarification if something is not understood
- Ask and answer questions in order to seek help, get information, or clarify something that is not understood

By grade 5, kids should:

- Engage effectively in a range of collaborative discussions (one-on-one, in groups, and teacher-led) with diverse partners on *grade 5 topics and texts*, building on others' ideas and expressing their own clearly
- Come to discussions prepared, having read or studied required material, and explicitly draw on that preparation and other information known about the topic to explore ideas under discussion
- Follow agreed-upon rules for discussions and carry out assigned roles
- Pose and respond to specific questions by making comments that contribute to the discussion and elaborate on the remarks of others
- Review the key ideas expressed and draw conclusions in light of information and knowledge gained from the discussions
- Summarize a written text read aloud or information presented in diverse media and formats, including visually, quantitatively, and orally
- Summarize the points a speaker makes and explain how each claim is supported by reasons and evidence

And, by grades 11 and 12, students are required to:

- Initiate and participate effectively in a range of collaborative discussions (one-on-one, in groups, and teacher-led) with diverse partners on *grade 11–12 topics, texts, and issues,* building on others' ideas and expressing their own clearly and persuasively
- Come to discussions prepared, having read and researched material under study, and explicitly draw on that preparation by referring to evidence from texts and other research on the topic or issue to stimulate a thoughtful, well-reasoned exchange of ideas

- Work with peers to promote civil, democratic discussions and decision making, set clear goals and deadlines, and establish individual roles as needed

- Propel conversations by posing and responding to questions that probe reasoning and evidence; ensure a hearing for a full range of positions on a topic or issue; clarify, verify, or challenge ideas and conclusions; and promote divergent and creative perspectives

- Respond thoughtfully to diverse perspectives; synthesize comments, claims, and evidence made on all sides of an issue; resolve contradictions when possible; and determine what additional information or research is required to deepen the investigation or complete the task

- Integrate multiple sources of information presented in diverse formats and media (e.g., visually, quantitatively, orally) in order to make informed decisions and solve problems, evaluating the credibility and accuracy of each source and noting any discrepancies among the data

- Evaluate a speaker's point of view, reasoning, and use of evidence and rhetoric; assess the stance, premises, links among ideas, word choice, points of emphasis, and tone used

Now we're talking real "college and career readiness." While critics complain that some CCSS targets are irrelevant or archaic, these goals couldn't be more appropriate and realistic.

Now we're talking real "college and career readiness." While critics complain that some CCSS targets are irrelevant or archaic, the above goals couldn't be more appropriate and realistic. School graduates who have mastered these speaking and listening skills are going to be miles ahead in their later studies, in career achievement, and in life.

Given that forty-five states initially adopted these guidelines, the CCSS has given the explicit teaching of social-academic skills a huge push. Even though a few states never joined up or have recently parted company with the national standards, each of those states has its own set of targets that are often very similar to the CCSS. For example, the Texas standards require fifth graders to "participate in student-led discussions by eliciting and considering suggestions from other group members and by identifying points of agreement and disagreement." And in high school, to "work productively with others in teams, building on the ideas of others, contributing relevant information, developing a plan for consensus-building, and setting ground rules for decision-making" (Texas Essential Knowledge and Skills, 2008).

Concern About School Climate, Violence, and Bullying

The socioemotional climate of our public schools and the relationships among the people who inhabit them have populated the headlines in recent years. The horrific school shootings, like those at Columbine and Sandy Hook, remind us that our schools are too often crime scenes, not safe harbors. And while the rate of major violence in U.S. schools has actually been shrinking since 1993, there are still ample reasons to worry about kids' safety.

The Centers for Disease Control (2013) reports that in a nationally representative sample of youth in grades 9–12:

- 12 percent reported being in a physical fight on school property in the twelve months before the survey.

- 5.9 percent reported that they did not go to school on one or more days in the thirty days before the survey because they felt unsafe at school or on their way to or from school.

- 5.4 percent reported carrying a weapon (gun, knife, or club) on school property on one or more days in the thirty days before the survey.

- 7.4 percent reported being threatened or injured with a weapon on school property one or more times in the twelve months before the survey.

- 20 percent reported being bullied on school property and 16 percent reported being bullied electronically during the twelve months before the survey.

- During 2010, there were about 828,000 nonfatal acts of violence at school among students ages twelve to eighteen.

- Approximately 7 percent of teachers reported that they had been threatened with injury or physically attacked by a student from their school.

- In 2009, about 20 percent of students ages twelve to eighteen reported that gangs were present at their school during the school year.

As the CDC wrapped up in its report:

> Not all injuries are visible. Exposure to youth violence and school violence can lead to a wide array of negative health behaviors and outcomes, including alcohol and drug use and suicide. Depression, anxiety, and many other psychological problems, including fear, can result from school violence. (Centers for Disease Control, 2013)

Among all these issues, bullying has been prioritized as a topic of urgent action. In fact, many states now require that each public school district have a bullying prevention program in place.

Concern also is growing about teenage suicide. According to the American Psychological Association (APA), teen suicide is the third-leading cause of death for young people ages fifteen to twenty-four, surpassed only by homicide and accidents. The CDC reports that each year, 20 percent of high school students seriously consider suicide, 14 percent make a plan, and 8 percent make a suicide attempt. What pushes certain kids over the edge? The APA offers an explanation:

> The risk for suicide frequently occurs in combination with external circumstances that seem to overwhelm at-risk teens who are unable to cope with the challenges of adolescence because of predisposing vulnerabilities such as mental disorders. Examples of stressors are disciplinary problems, interpersonal losses, family violence, sexual orientation confusion, physical and sexual abuse and being the victim of bullying. (American Psychological Association, 2013)

Discriminatory Discipline Practices

Many traditional school disciplinary policies have now been shown to be unfair to some groups of students. Both governmental and private research studies have shown that minority students are disproportionately excluded from school through a wide array of disciplinary practices: corporal punishment, suspension, expulsion, and even referrals to police and arrests. For example, compared to white students, black students were twice as likely to face corporal punishment; 2.5 times as likely to be suspended in or out of school or arrested in a school-related incident; three times as likely to be expelled; and four times as likely to face out-of-school suspension multiple times. Similarly, Native American students were twice as likely as white students to be suspended from school several times, expelled, referred to law enforcement or arrested, or face corporal punishment (American Institutes for Research, 2013).

All these factors combine to keep minority students out of their seats in classrooms, losing instructional time, falling behind their peers, and becoming ever more likely to drop out of schools without the skills to support themselves, and thus feeding today's accelerated, school-to-prison pipeline. In response to these accumulating reports, Secretary of Education Arne Duncan went to Howard University to pledge action:

> Perhaps the most alarming findings involve the topic of discipline. The sad fact is that minority students across America face much harsher discipline than nonminorities, even within the same school. Some examples—African American students, particularly males, are far more likely to be suspended or expelled from school than their peers. (Holland, 2012)

These data are not new. Reports about inequities in school discipline policies have been circulating for decades (Skiba et al., 2002). Some cities, like Baltimore, have been revising their suspension policies to keep kids in school and learning. Since 2000, Baltimore has moved to in-school discipline approaches, and therefore lowered its suspension rate by 58 percent (Cichan, 2012). Other districts and states are finally experimenting with a variety of fairer and less exclusionary discipline approaches, including restorative justice, teen court, and peer mediation.

Best Practice Instruction Requires Social-Academic Skills

Although the term *best practice* is often used with vague intent, decades of thoughtful research have yielded a clear consensus on what optimal classroom instruction looks like—and it doesn't look like kids sitting in straight rows of desks with their hands folded, listening to a teacher talk. Best practice teaching can only happen in a flexible, decentralized classroom where kids take action in a variety of configurations, assume responsibility, work with pride, hold themselves accountable, and support one another. In the fourth edition of their book *Best Practice: Bringing Standards to Life in America's Schools* (Zemelman, 2012), Harvey and co-authors Steve Zemelman and Art Hyde synthesize recent findings about the most effective pedagogies.

Drawing on the reports and recommendations from the whole range of education research centers, subject matter organizations, and standards-setting agencies, Zemelman, Daniels, and Hyde offer a model of powerful learning that is student-centered, cognitive, and interactive. This consensus vision of best practice can be summarized by looking at the following chart, which shows development from conventional toward more student-centered teaching.

As you can see, the interlocking conditions of good instruction cannot happen under the old command-and-control models of top-down school discipline. The new paradigm both requires and creates interdependence among everyone in the classroom. The characteristic structures and activities of state-of-the-art teaching require a pervasive climate of student self-awareness, autonomy, responsibility, collaboration, and reflection.

INDICATORS OF BEST PRACTICE

This chart illustrates movement from a teacher-directed to a student-centered classroom. Growth along this continuum does not mean complete abandonment of established instructional approaches. Instead, teachers add new alternatives to a widening repertoire of choices, allowing them to move among a richer array of activities, creating a more diverse and complex balance.

Classroom Setup: *Promotes Student Collaboration*

- Setup for teacher-centered instruction (separate desks) ▶ Student-centered arrangement (tables)

- Rows of desks ▶ Varied learning spaces for whole-class, small-group, and independent work

- Bare, unadorned space ▶ Commercial decorations ▶ Student-made artwork, products, displays of work

- Few materials ▶ Textbooks and handouts ▶ Varied resources (books, magazines, artifacts, manipulatives, etc.)

Classroom Climate: *Actively Involves Students*

- Management by consequences and rewards ▶ Order maintained by engagement and community

- Teacher creates and enforces rules ▶ Students help set and enforce norms

- Students are quiet, motionless, passive, controlled ▶ Students are responsive, active, purposeful, autonomous

- Fixed student grouping based on ability ▶ Flexible grouping based on tasks and choice

- Consistent, unvarying schedule ▶ Predictable but flexible time usage based on activities

Voice and Responsibility: *Balanced Between Teacher- and Student-Directed*

- Teacher relies solely on an established curriculum ▶ Some themes and inquiries are built from students' own questions ("negotiated curriculum")
- Teacher chooses all activities ▶ Students often select inquiry topics, books, writing topics, audiences, etc.
- Teacher directs all assignments ▶ Students assume responsibility, take roles in decision making, help run classroom life
- Whole-class reading and writing assignments ▶ Independent reading (SSR, reading workshop, or book clubs) and independent writing (journals, writing workshop)
- Teacher assesses, grades, and keeps all records ▶ Students maintain their own records, set own goals, self-assess

Language and Communication: *Deepen Learning*

- Silence ▶ Purposeful noise and conversation
- Short responses ▶ Elaborated discussion ▶ Students' own questions and evaluations
- Teacher talk ▶ Student–teacher talk ▶ Student–student talk plus teacher conferring with students
- Talk and writing focus on: Facts ▶ Skills ▶ Concepts ▶ Synthesis and reflection

Activities and Assignments: *Balance the Traditional and More Interactive*

- Teacher presents material ▶ Students read, write, and talk every day ▶ Students actively experience concepts
- Whole-class teaching ▶ Small-group instruction ▶ Wide variety of activities, balancing individual work, small groups, and whole-class activities
- Uniform curriculum for all ▶ Jigsawed curriculum (different but related topics, according to kids' needs or choices)
- Light coverage of wide range of subjects ▶ Intensive, deep study of selected topics
- Short-term lessons, one day at a time ▶ Extended activities; multiday, multistep projects
- Isolated subject lessons ▶ Integrated, thematic, cross-disciplinary inquiries
- Focus on memorization and recall of facts ▶ Focus on applying knowledge and problem solving
- Short responses, fill-in-the-blank exercises ▶ Complex responses, evaluations, writing, performances, artwork

- Identical assignments for all ▶ Differentiated curriculum for all styles and abilities

Student Work and Assessment: *Inform Teachers, Students, Parents*

- Products created for teachers and grading ▶ Products created for real events and audiences
- Classroom/hallway displays: no student work posted ▶ "A" papers only ▶ All students represented
- Identical, imitative products displayed ▶ Varied and original products displayed
- Teacher feedback via scores and grades ▶ Teacher feedback and conferences are substantive and formative
- Products are seen and rated only by teachers ▶ Public exhibitions and performances are common
- Data kept private in teacher gradebook ▶ Work kept in student-maintained portfolios
- All assessment by teachers ▶ Student self-assessment an official element ▶ Parents are involved
- Standards set during grading ▶ Standards available in advance ▶ Standards codeveloped with students

Teacher Attitude and Outlook: *Take Professional Initiative*

Relationship with students is:

- Distant, impersonal, fearful ▶ Positive, warm, respectful, encouraging
- Judging ▶ Understanding, empathizing, inquiring, guiding
- Directive ▶ Consultative

Attitude toward self is:

- Powerless worker ▶ Risk taker/experimenter ▶ Creative, active professional
- Solitary adult ▶ Member of team with other adults in school ▶ Member of networks beyond school
- Staff development recipient ▶ Director of own professional growth

View of role is:

- Expert, presenter, gatekeeper ▶ Coach, mentor, model, guide

Teachers Need Support in Teaching Social-Academic Skills

Most of us went to school under an authoritarian discipline system. Why would we feel comfortable or eager to depart from the paradigm on which we were raised?

Even as the call for social-emotional learning grows louder, teachers aren't exactly leaping forward to lead the movement. This is not just because state officials, school reformers, and publishers got a jump-start (though they did). We teachers, let's not forget, were students once too, and we didn't necessarily encounter good teaching around social skills, either. Most of us went to school (and future teachers are still attending school) under an authoritarian discipline system. We didn't have much experience with approaches other than rules, rewards, and punishments. Why would we feel comfortable or eager to depart from the paradigm on which we were raised, especially considering how well *we* turned out? (And it is worth recognizing that most of us eventual teachers were "good kids," who didn't run afoul of the discipline system enough to taste its harshest lash.)

In our workshops, we often ask teachers to think back on their own experiences with collaborative, partner, or group work in school. Many simply laugh and say, "I hated it!" The most painful problem they recollect is that, when working in small groups, they always had to do the majority of the work to ensure their own good grade, carrying the slackers to the finish line on their own bent backs. We now realize that these folks, so many of today's teachers, were victims of ill-structured cooperative learning, and carry negative attitudes and misconceptions about students working together. And even if we later got some formal training in proper collaborative learning, it may have been be too brief and weak to overcome those early negative experiences. So, if we are going to be required to explicitly teach social-academic skills, we need more support, training, and materials than we've been offered so far.

But it gets even more personal. Some states—Illinois, for one—are adopting teacher assessment rubrics that assign points for classrooms that feature well-structured student collaboration, discussion, and debate. These ranking systems reward teachers who successfully incorporate such interaction into their daily teaching—and punish those who don't. For example, the widely used Charlotte Danielson teacher evaluation rubric requires kids to be working cooperatively in order for their teacher to receive the highest possible "Distinguished" ranking. In her rationale, Danielson writes:

> As important as a teacher's treatment of students is, how students are treated by their classmates is arguably even more important to students. At its worst, poor treatment causes students to feel rejected by their peers. At its best, positive interactions among students are mutually supportive and create an emotionally healthy school environment. Teachers not only model and teach students how to engage in respectful interactions with one another but also acknowledge such interaction. (Danielson, 2011)

With salaries and even continued employment now depending on one-time evaluations like these, teachers better have an interactive community humming when the principal comes around to score them.

Bottom line: the world is asking teachers to run their classrooms in new ways, but it hasn't yet provided the practical tools they need to make such large and sometimes uncomfortable changes.

Emerging Research:
Social-Emotional Skills *Can* Be Taught

There is a robust and growing body of research that validates the explicit teaching of social-academic skills. Earlier, we cited the Durlak meta-analysis, which showed remarkable academic gains for kids who had been taught key social skills. The Chicago-based Collaborative for Academic, Social, and Emotional Learning (CASEL) is dedicated to collecting and disseminating scientifically based evidence of "what works" in social-emotional learning. A thorough listing of current studies, along with effectiveness rankings for many of the commercial programs currently for sale, can be found at www.casel.org.

Today's most commonly used teacher evaluation rubric requires kids to be working cooperatively in order for their teacher to receive the highest possible "Distinguished" ranking.

A variety of researchers have looked closely at the relationship between school climate and student achievement. Evidence consistently ties poor socioemotional climates to low achievement and test scores. In its *School Climate Research Summary,* the National School Climate Center summarizes recent findings:

> School climate matters. Positive and sustained school climate is associated with and/or predictive of positive child and youth development, effective risk prevention and health promotion efforts, student learning and academic achievement, increased student graduation rates, and teacher retention. (Thapa et al., 2012)

One related line of inquiry comes out of the Consortium for Chicago Schools Research at the University of Chicago. Over a series of studies, Anthony Bryk and colleagues have shown that "relational trust is the 'glue' or the essential element" that potentiates all the other factors leading to school improvement (Bryk et al., 2010; Bryk & Schneider, 2002). In other words, in schools that cultivate friendliness and mutual support, kids learn better.

It is important to note that in addition to general studies of social-emotional learning, investigations in separate academic disciplines cross-validate these findings. For example, the pioneering literacy researcher Richard Allington has shown that when students regularly discuss their reading with peers, gains are seen in engagement, in comprehension, and on high-stakes reading tests (2012). In the mathematics world, similar connections have been found between social-emotional skills and academic achievement. In several studies, researchers at the Yale Child Study Center found strong links between social competencies and academic achievement. As the investigators reported, "the strengths of the relationships between students' knowledge of themselves and others and their achievement in math was found to be strong" (Haynes et al., 2003).

My Kids, Right Now

There's one more reason why we need to teach social skills in our classrooms: this is our *life*. We are in real classrooms today, each of us with a group of kids (or five groups of kids), in some kind of relationship, for nine months. For everyone's morale, sense of safety, hunger for belonging, and need to take risks and grow, we must create a friendly, supportive place to be. We want everyone to walk through that classroom door with smiles on their faces this morning, acknowledging and savoring our differences, feeling our solidarity, and feeding off one another's energy.

We are complicated and separate people, and we'll bring some junk through that door too, but if we address our interaction forthrightly and practice sociable behavior together, we can dial down the static, put aside our baggage, and grow with our friends' support. Instead of cutting each other down, we can all stand on each other's shoulders. In the game of school, we can enjoy Home Court Advantage every day. And we would prefer this to happen *right now*.

How to Address These Problems and Seize the Opportunities

In this resource, we offer thirty-five classroom-ready lessons that address this whole array of problems and opportunities. These lessons

- Are all directly correlated with the Common Core standards for Speaking and Listening
- Engage students in experiences that systematically build a sense of belonging and personal significance
- Make kids feel safer and more connected, so they are less likely to put down or bully others
- Enable highly interactive, student-driven best practice instruction to succeed in your classroom
- Help you feel comfortable and ready to tackle this new teaching task—and enjoy the challenge
- Get you ready to be assessed in your own classroom, by showcasing students who work together fluidly, flexibly, and with focus
- Ground you with a strong research and knowledge base in the emerging field of social-emotional learning, as well as related and longer-established fields of inquiry
- Help you grow or mend your classroom climate *now*, to solve management and morale problems, and develop long-term spirit and solidarity
- Make sure all your students acquire the social-*academic* skills they need for their future education, and in their lives as workers, community members, and citizens

All Social Skills Programs Are Not Alike

In today's crowded school marketplace, there are countless programs promising to teach social, or emotional, or behavior, or collaboration, or interpersonal skills. We deeply respect a number of them; Responsive Classroom, Facing History, the Child Development Center, Restorative Justice, and others do wonderful, pro-social work. Some other SEL programs are based on adult-dictated rules, warnings, contingent rewards, and swift punishments. Not to put too fine a point on it, obedience-driven discipline is still very much in the driver's seat in this market segment.

One of the most widely adopted SEL programs, Second Step, comes with a teacher kit of highly scripted lessons. Second Step's parent organization, the Committee for Children, identifies the core skill of its program as "self-regulation":

> In a nutshell, self-regulation is the ability to monitor and manage emotions, thoughts, and behaviors. It's what helps students focus their attention on a lesson when they may be distracted by noisy classmates, a problem they had at recess, or excitement about an upcoming birthday party. (Committee for Children, 2011)

God forbid that a child should have an outburst of delight over a birthday!

We're not disputing the reality that in this culture, the habit of self-control and the mind-set of delayed gratification contribute to certain kinds of success. But many of the SEL programs we've studied stifle children's genuine emotions, swapping immediate gratification for immediate obedience. This movement cannot be called an innovation if social-emotional learning becomes a backdoor route to old-school discipline: shut the kids up, sit them down, and maintain an emotionally flat tone in school, day in and day out.

Other SEL programs trade the iron fist of self-regulation for the velvet glove of psychobabble. A long and balanced piece on the SEL movement in the *New York Times* reports from one kindergarten classroom (Kahn, 2013). The teacher invites kids to tell about problems with their parents. When one boy admits that his mother yelled at him, the teacher imitates a screaming parent and encourages the child to think up an answer to his angry mother. Finally, the kid manages, "Mommy, I don't like it when you scream at me." The teacher approvingly predicts, "And maybe your Mommy will say, 'I'm sorry.'" But then again, maybe Mommy won't appreciate such backtalk, and things at home could escalate.

Education Week ran another generally admiring piece on social-emotional learning (Heitlin, 2013). In one lesson, fifth graders are asked to use markers and paper to draw pictures of their own faces. Then, the teacher reads aloud a story full of anger and put-downs. At each negative turn in the story, she instructs kids to tear off a part of their own face from the pictures they have created. Before the story is done, much of the class is in tears.

We mention these worrisome examples not to condemn the whole SEL movement, of which we are a part, but to caution against uncritical adoption of programs with foreseeably damaging consequences. And also to say: *this is not what we do.* Though we are definitely psychological in our outlook, we do not promote (or condone) classroom group therapy, behavior modification, psychodrama, or emotional blackmail.

Researchers at the Yale Child Study Center found strong links between social competencies and academic achievement.

What is vanishingly rare today is a program that actually *shows kids* what good behavior looks like, *explicitly teaches* it, and provides *closely guided practice* so that young people can actually acquire new ways of acting and interacting. That's what this resource aims to do.

We are living in a world of *standards.* So let us propose one: every student in your classroom works with every other kid, regularly, cheerfully, and supportively, all year long. No one says, "I won't work with her." That's a standard we want to help you meet.

Our Theory of Action

So what is our own theoretical background, what are our assumptions and our research base? The next short chapter gives you that information in more detail.

Here's a preview: We come out of the worlds of social psychology, group dynamics, and collaborative learning. We grow kids' social-academic skills not by limiting, coercing, or controlling them, but by offering them *more* responsibility, control, and choice. We treat them like the people they want to become. We take it as our responsibility to model the behaviors that we want kids to practice. We provide explicit demonstrations, guided practice, close coaching, feedback, and systematic reflection. Our theory of action is this: acquaintance leads to friendship, which in turn leads to supportive behavior. In the classroom community that *you can create*, kids predictably acquire individual and collaborative social strategies that become automatic, that serve them today in school and onward through their lives.

And one other thing: these lessons are fun. Kids love them.

Chapter 2

Theory and Research on Social-Academic Skills Training

What kind of teaching nightmares scare you in the middle of night? Nancy wakes up in a cold sweat attempting to escape the class from hell: kids who won't stay in their seats, ignore her stimulating lesson plans, swear when asked to put their phones away, and storm out of the room whenever they feel like it. Smokey quakes at the very real memory of John Ross, who jumped out of his second-story classroom window after being rebuked for misbehavior by his rookie teacher. (It turned out to be a well-planned prank, no injuries.) So, when it comes to teaching, we've seen (or dreamed) it all.

Teaching is hard, hard work, and often the kids are predictable in their unpredictability. And what seems like a best practice lesson to us can be rewarded with loud yawns, blank stares, and an intense and exclusive conversation with the friend in the next row. Once in a while we try groups, and those same kids who disrupted class before are now merrily leading whole groups of kids off course, off task, off lesson. In response, we retreat to whole-class instruction because it just seems safer. But now this whole Social and Emotional Learning movement is breathing down our necks. Like it isn't tough enough just to teach our content without now having the responsibility of teaching the kids how to be civil, thoughtful human beings as well!

Though programs and practices in the SEL movement range from exemplary to dubious (see pages 12–14), the conditions warranting SEL are inarguable:

- The Common Core State Standards define College and Career Readiness in both academic and social terms. While all students must be able to defend their arguments with supporting text details, they've also got to be able to listen carefully, add to ideas, show respect, and disagree civilly (CCSS, 2010).

- More and more states are adopting SEL standards, which typically include three skill elements: Self-Awareness and Self-Management, Social and Interpersonal Awareness, and Decision-Making and Responsible Behaviors (Performance Descriptors, 2003).

Students with SEL skills perform better academically. Students with such training averaged 11 percentile points higher on achievement tests than did students without training.

Research shows that the *most effective social skill* training for kids is not gigantic, school-wide programs, but simple classroom teacher-led programs.

- While schools place great importance on academic skills, employers place equal emphasis on communication, collaboration, critical and creative thinking, ingenuity, innovation, and risk taking (Carter, 2013).

- When polled, year after year, around 66 percent of high school students report they are bored at school every day (Yazzie-Mintz, 2009).

- Students with SEL skills perform better academically. Students with such training averaged 11 percentile points higher on achievement tests than did students without training (Durlak et al., 2011).

- Improved social and emotional skills decrease disruptive classroom behavior (Weissberg & Cascarino, 2013).

Hey, did you catch those last two items? When kids are socially skilled, they can learn better and behave better. So maybe some form of SEL is a way for us to begin living our alternative teacher dream, the one where the kids follow directions, treat others with respect, and take ownership of their learning.

Now, here is the really interesting part: research shows that the *most effective social skill* training for kids is not gigantic, school-wide programs, but simple classroom teacher-led programs (Durlak et al., 2011). We repeat: what we teachers do in the classroom can have a bigger positive impact on our students' behaviors and their test scores than many mandated, packaged programs.

Research Base

We have known all this for a long, long time. Reflecting over 1,200 studies, cooperative learning—which is to say, *the explicit teaching of social skills in group settings*—is probably the single best-researched and most effective innovation in education in the last half-century (Johnson & Johnson, 2009). It is based on social psychology research dating back to Kurt Lewin's 1940 discovery of a phenomenon he named *group dynamics*. Lewin defined group dynamics as the way small groups and individuals react to and interact with one another. His key insight was that groups were not just a combination of their component individuals, but a different, far more complex entity. In trying to explain the power and potential of human groups, Lewin actually coined the phrase, "The whole is greater than the sum of its parts."

Morton Deutsch continued Lewin's research by examining how the behaviors of people within a social group are interrelated. What both Lewin and Deutsch discovered is that no human group is ever static. Members can *change* the dynamics by changing their individual behaviors. This revelation sparked attempts to harness the positive power of groups in school settings, resulting in a model called cooperative learning. Led by researchers like Schlomo Saharan, David Johnson, Roger Johnson, Robert Slavin, and others, early cooperative learning models were able to prove how the efforts of people working in groups— like students studying school subjects—could be maximized. (For more about the seventy-five-year research base on social skills development in schools, see the reading list at the end of this book.)

While cooperative learning is significantly more effective than individual or competitive learning approaches (Johnson & Johnson, 2009), it is also challenging to implement: it requires teachers to reframe their own roles. When we set out to teach social and collaboration skills, we need to be not just tellers, but models and coaches—we really do need to become a "guide on the side" versus a "sage on the stage." Very predictably, when teachers first introduce cooperative learning to their kids, the initial student groups don't always work very well. Why? Well, we can blame the kids' bad upbringing, but in actuality, collaborative work can flop because learning *anything* new takes time to master. We teachers can be pretty impatient when it comes to an imperfect lesson—and we feel under a lot of pressure to deliver quick results, especially these days. So we may bail out before we've given kids enough time, practice, and feedback to add new behaviors to their social repertoire. Also, as often happens in schools, our district's support for social skills training may suddenly evaporate, leaving teachers scanning the horizon for the next top-down mandate from the central office.

Very predictably, when teachers first introduce cooperative learning to their kids, the initial student groups don't always work very well.

But hey, instead of retreating from the challenges of teaching student collaboration, let's examine the obstacles. We know many of them first hand.

Recollections

Think about your first years of teaching. If they were like ours, you often felt frustrated. We both remember putting students into groups of four or five, hoping for some academic discussion that reflected deep thinking, attentive listening, and careful consideration of one another's viewpoints. Instead, we watched groups quickly career off task, break up into subgroups, or—even worse—completely ignore one member. Superficial but dutiful conversations would ramp up when we entered a group's gravitational field, about four or five feet away. But when we orbited further out, topics reverted to soccer, music, and who's dating who. It seemed like every time we tried a great group activity, it somehow fell flat. Some groups clicked and others clacked. The net benefit felt nil. Disappointed yet again, we would return to what "worked": teacher-directed, whole-class instruction.

Only later, through our study of group dynamics as well as the Johnson brothers' model of cooperative learning, did we understand the planning and decisions that must be made ahead of time in order to get groups to truly collaborate. And hey, guess what? The research almost immediately addressed one of our mistakes: we were making the groups too large! That's why you'll notice that most of our lessons in the beginning part of this book focus on pairs: pairs are easier for students and teachers to manage successfully.

Our guess is that you've experienced the same student collaboration frustrations that we did. If you think more broadly about your own development as a teacher, your comfort and agility increased as your experience enabled you to anticipate potential problems and then prevent them. You found ways to build a more positive classroom community. You became increasingly adept at managing the unforeseen, right on the spot. Perhaps you found a mentor teacher, someone who affirmed your efforts and offered some caring assistance in solving the problems that stumped you. Along the way, most of us attended at least one cooperative learning or collaboration workshop. However, once the training was over, we needed more tangible implementation support than a certificate of attendance. We hope that this book and its accompanying slides will provide the classroom follow-up that most of us never got.

Back in the 1990s, Nancy became a high-level trainer in the Johnson and Johnson cooperative learning model. She attended advanced training in Minnesota with the Johnson brothers, and became a teacher–leader back home in Chicago. Besides offering colleagues a full week of teacher training in the summer, Nancy also provided monthly follow-up workshops that focused on problem solving, strategizing, and celebration. From all of those staff development encounters with peers, Nancy grew to anticipate the predictable problems those moving from sage to guide would encounter. Today, from our almost-too-many decades of working with kids and educators, we want to offer you the full support you need to bring friendly, supportive, interactive, and collaborative behaviors to life in your classroom.

Starting With a Partner

The simplest way to keep students on task is to put them in pairs. That's the reason why all of the lessons in our first three families use partners. Why are pairs so productive? First, when students are working in partners, the overall engagement level is high; 50 percent of the group members are talking about the material at any given moment. Second, it's easy for students to manage working in pairs, even if they have little collaboration experience. In a pair, all you have to do is pay attention to one person. You don't have to skillfully include others. You don't have to listen carefully in order to combine various ideas. You are less likely to completely monopolize a conversation. Plus, pairs can work quickly. Think about your own committee work: the bigger the committee, the longer everything takes.

> If you notice student groups getting distracted by others, look at how the furniture is arranged, how close the kids are sitting, and where the members are facing.

The other great thing about pairs is that they are easy to monitor, particularly when partners are sitting side by side. We like to call this arrangement "shoulder partners," as opposed to "face partners," who are sitting across from each other. The very first lesson (page 40) focuses on forming shoulder partners. Though this lesson only takes a couple of minutes, it's critical for classroom management. When students pair up correctly, the furniture is neither impeding interaction, nor is it blocking your ability to get around the room easily and quickly. A cornerstone of on-task behavior is teaching groups how to sit as close together as possible. The closer that partners sit together, the better they can focus on each other and ignore other students in the room. So here's a quick tip: if you notice student groups getting distracted by others, look at how the furniture is arranged, how close the kids are sitting, and where the members are facing. Students with a goal of talking to members of other groups will position their bodies at angles that make off-task conversations easy and convenient. Incorrect seating also sends this message to a partner: "I'm not interested in you or what you have to say."

By now you are probably wondering, "Don't you ever use groups larger than pairs?" Yes, we do, but before we choose a group larger than a pair we ask this question: Why do we need to use a larger group? Of course, there are lots of good reasons: the text is jigsawed, the discussion needs multiple voices, or the project is multifaceted. We're certain you can think of others. However, if we can't think of a really good reason to use a larger group, we stick with pairs.

When you do choose larger student groups, we don't recommend a size above four unless you have a high absence rate and can reliably count on that fifth member being absent. The same set-up rules apply whether using pairs or larger groups: members need to move the furniture so that they can sit as close together as possible, fully face one another, and screen out visual and auditory distractions from other groups. As we mentioned earlier, chairs turned only partway and sideways seating are purposeful off-task conversation postures. Don't hesitate to help members of a group stand up and reposition the furniture so that you can monitor them more easily and so that they will stay better focused on one another. Learning how to form groups correctly with inhospitable furniture and tight conditions is another skill to master. In addition, you'll notice that we save larger groups for later lessons because they require a greater repertoire of interpersonal skills—skills that will have to be explicitly taught and then practiced regularly.

Building a Community of Acquaintance

Our core belief is that kids must get to know each other deeply and personally. The second lesson in this book is the Partner Interview, which invites pairs of kids to take turns sharing personal experiences, interests, and opinions. And later, when larger groups meet, we use a version of this acquaintance-building activity called the Membership Grid. For the first five minutes of a group meeting, students share their experiences and stories on a low-risk topic. This peer chitchat may sound superficial, but those short conversations enable students to build working friendships. Think about a group you belong to that has high productivity and high morale. Chances are, people enjoy friendly relationships and regularly share personal information and stories with each other (think wedding pictures, movie recommendations, district gossip).

These icebreaking conversations also give students the simple license to get to know more classmates. Most kids aren't good at spontaneous mingling, and we think they become increasingly reticent and self-conscious as they get older. Friendship circles can get ossified for years, and kids don't actually expand their networks. Nancy remembers her sophomore year in chemistry. She had the same lab partner all year, but never had a single conversation with him. They did the labs and completed the work, but following the lab instructions never provided an opening for them to get to know each other.

Building acquaintance is important for many reasons. First, it's harder to be mean to people you know. Why do you think all of those trolls feel free to scutter around the Internet, spewing their bile? The reason is simple: anonymity.

Changing partners frequently gives kids permission to talk to people who are different than they are, which in turn helps them realize that those people aren't really so different; they just thought they were.

Few students truly want to be considered mean, but when you don't know someone, it's a lot easier to ignore them or disregard their feelings. Plus, we are more accountable to those we know. Many times, a group member's off-task behavior stems from a lack of acquaintance. It is easy to let strangers down without feeling very guilty. Second, students need to function in a diverse world. Given a choice, kids will stick with their friends. And you know what? Adults do the same thing. Go to a conference and see how many friends split up at the door in order to meet new people. They don't. Changing partners frequently gives kids permission to talk to people who are different than they are, which in turn helps them realize that those people aren't really so different; they just thought they were. Finally, when you get to know people, you are a lot more interested in what they think. Any discussion is only as good as how interested the members are in one another's ideas. And the corollary of this is that students who are interested in each other's ideas will be more likely to take the risk and share their own thoughts.

Building a Community of Respect, Inclusion, and Gratefulness

Other lessons in the beginning of this resource focus exclusively on how students need to treat each other. The first lesson that bridges this concept is Home Court; its goal is to help curtail put-downs that students thinly disguise as humor. The next lesson explicitly teaches the social skill of Friendliness and Support. Though this seems like a skill everyone should enter school knowing, it is often absent. Students may offer friendliness and support to their closest pals, but even then much of it is implied versus spoken. We want kids to use friendliness and support much more vigorously and widely. When someone in your group comes up with an interesting idea you never thought of, you tell them! Explicitly expressing appreciation for the unique skills and ideas of others shows members they are valued. When members are valued, respect and inclusion are part of the package.

Something else you will notice in our lessons is that most of them end with group members thanking one another. Though some might view this as being prescriptive and artificial, our classroom experience shows that kids don't often thank people for their efforts; nor do they get thanked for their own. We think students do often appreciate the work of their classmates—and their teachers— but it never occurs to them to voice it. That's something we want to change. Thanking people for their efforts builds a positive community. People who feel appreciated want to return to a group and work together again. Just the other day, an article on gratefulness appeared in the *Wall Street Journal*. Titled "Raising Children With an Attitude of Gratitude: Research Finds Real Benefits for Kids Who Say 'Thank You,'" the article pointed out that kids who thank others and feel grateful have a more positive attitude toward school and life, and—wait for it—higher GPAs (Kapp, 2013). On the flip side, kids who spend their time inventorying their gripes have lower grades and higher rates of depression, envy, and general dissatisfaction. The article also pointed out that kids need to be taught to be thankful; it needs to be modeled and practiced. According to the article, "Gratitude works like a muscle." The more you flex it, the more grateful you feel. That means we teachers are personal trainers!

Taking Personal Responsibility

When students meet with their groups, they need to be consciously assessing themselves at the three different junctures. First, *prior to a meeting*, a member needs to actively decide:

- What do I need to do in order to get ready for this meeting and be a full contributor? And how am I going to make sure this preparation gets done in time?

Thanking people for their efforts builds a positive community. People who feel appreciated want to return to a group and work together again.

Sometimes, members have the opportunity to complete the work right in class directly before a meeting. (We've structured this book's lessons this way, so that they can mostly unfold in one class period or less.) However, as students move up through the grades, this responsibility for preparation takes the form of homework. If students are in literature circles, each member needs to read the chosen chapters and prepare discussion notes. If students are in writing circles, each member needs to come to the group with a piece of writing ready to share. If students are working on a research project, each member needs to take responsibility for completing certain components by the time of the next meeting.

The second responsibility juncture occurs *during the meeting*. At this point, a proficient collaborator is asking three questions:

- How are my contributions going to make an academic difference to this meeting?
- What skills must I use to help the group function on a high level?
- How can I learn from the other members of this group?

And then, *when a meeting concludes*, each individual must begin to plan for the next meeting:

- How can I be more skillful in my contributions and my interactions?
- What might I do differently so that I can learn more from the rest of my group?
- What do I need to do in order to get ready for the next meeting?

As students work together, we use the occasion to develop a culture of personal responsibility. Students need to be able to articulate how they are contributing to the group and how they are helping others to contribute as well. They also need to understand the negative impact of not being prepared, not thinking ahead, or not setting goals for improvement. That's taking personal responsibility.

Whenever people groan at the mention of groups, it is probably because they have been trapped in groups whose members didn't take responsibility. Every so often, you'll run across articles deriding teamwork as a useless waste of time prone to circular brainstorming, unimaginative thinking, and collaborative inhibition. However, when you read these articles carefully, it turns out that these teams are failing because the personal responsibility expectations are unclear. For any high-level group to fully function, members need to come with their best contributions in hand and their best interpersonal skills at the ready. This means that a work group must have clear goals and expectations for individual members, just as a student group would.

Teaching Interpersonal Skills Explicitly

Students need to be able to articulate how they are contributing to the group and how they are helping others to contribute as well.

Most students do not come to us equipped with all the skills they need to function in a group. However, since we are teachers, we can *teach* them those skills and then have kids *practice* them every time they work together. But sometimes teachers feel reluctant to explicitly teach interpersonal skills. Some find it a little too "touchy-feely." Others cling to a romantic view of their content: engaging curricular material by itself should be enough to generate good small-group interactions. And then there are those who are waiting for the right kids to come along, the ones who already have the skills when they show up in September.

If you feel any of these types of reluctance, we recommend that you push them all aside and try a few explicit social-academic lessons. Once you've begun, this will feel like smart classroom management, not a squishy sidetrack. You'll no longer be waiting for the right kids to show up, because you'll be making sure you have "a good group" every year. And, thanks to that training, your highly engaging curriculum material *will* create great discussion, because the kids are going to have the skills to work with it!

Stages of Learning Social Skills

If you look over our interpersonal skill lessons, you'll notice that they all follow a similar format. Getting kids to buy into a skill starts with getting them to recognize a need for it. Then we ask students to imagine the following: How would a group function if they used that skill? What kind of body language might an observer see? What would members say to one another? Finally, students get to practice the new behavior with their partners or groups. This practice is what takes some time. Learning a new skill moves through four predictable stages (Johnson, Johnson, & Holubec, 2008).

1. Discomfort and Avoidance. Actually saying things like "That was a great answer; I didn't think of that" will feel weird and unnatural to students who have never before vocalized friendliness and support to their peers. At first, students will attempt to avoid using a skill and may even argue about it because it makes them uncomfortable. Keep in mind, the harder kids resist, the more they need that skill. In response to that resistance, just smile patiently and insist that you're not leaving until you hear some specific skill statements from the group. At that point the members will give in because they want to get rid of you. Once you've heard the skill, compliment them enthusiastically and move on.

2. Phony Use. If you have persevered, your students have given up the fight. Now, when you drop by the group, they collectively go, "Uh-oh, better whip out that skill she wants us to use." As you observe, members will say the same rote phrase every time anyone says anything. It would be nice if they could expand their repertoire, but the kids are still a bit uncomfortable. But at least you didn't have to prod them this time! Celebrate their improved skillfulness and move on.

3. Overuse. At this stage, group members have finally bought into the skill. As a matter of fact, now it's kind of fun—sort of an in-joke. They challenge one another to see who can use every phrase on the class list. They high five every other minute. To the outsider this might all appear kind of goofy, but the group members have discovered that they really do have more fun and enjoy one another when they use these skills. Be happy when they mock the process. High five the groups and compliment them on their extreme skill usage!

4. Integrated Use. When students reach this stage, they are using the skill appropriately and automatically. They don't need to stop and think, "I'd better use this skill." Instead, when they hear another member say something really interesting, "Wow, I didn't even think of that!" just pops right out. It takes a long time for students to get to this final stage. But the more opportunity students have to work together and the more you encourage their practicing the skill, the quicker they'll achieve proficiency!

After the initial introduction of a skill, the best way to shepherd its mastery is to keep insisting the kids use it, day after day, meeting after meeting.

Positive Interdependence

Students should only be working in groups if it will enhance the task and the learning. Never put students together if a task could be completed just as well individually. That's one of the reasons why we insist on students preparing their discussion notes individually. We want them to take the time to think deeply and gather their own unique thoughts about the content. When students prepare for a discussion together, face-to-face, they often end up bringing fewer new ideas to the group. Plus, working together at this stage often produces the kind of "collaborative inhibition" that teamwork naysayers frequently cite. Rather than disagreeing or challenging ideas, the less confident (or hitchhiking) student will typically respond, "That's a good question. I'm going to put that down too. What else did you think of?" Remember, for groups to function at a high level, personal responsibility must also run high, and that begins with bringing your share of ideas to the group. Groups will thrive when everyone feels like all members are doing their share of the work.

Students should only be working in groups if it will enhance the task and the learning.

How does positive interdependence occur when a group does meet face-to-face?

First, **the group's task cannot be completed alone.** Members need one another to get the job done. It's hard to have a discussion with yourself.

Second, **the group is responsible for specific learning goals.** Toward the end of a meeting, our lessons often include each group sharing its most interesting discussion item. We always recommend that you call on members at random rather than having groups designate a member to report back. Groups need to understand that everybody must be able to articulate the information to others.

A group discussion is a chance to share observations and challenge ideas, but it is also an opportunity to rehearse the presentation of the group's learning accomplishments.

Third, groups must work together in order to refine their interaction skills. These are the skills that you've explicitly taught and are now reminding them to use.

Reflection and Celebration

At the end of a discussion, students need to stop and assess their interactions. When groups are first meeting, we like to emphasize what went well. We ask, "What were three things your group did that got the job done and enabled you to get along?" Groups that explicitly and regularly highlight their successes look forward to the next meeting and bond more quickly because this celebration enhances friendship and the common desire to work well as a team. After a couple of meetings, we continue to inventory the positives, but we also begin asking, "What's something you could do better the next time?"

At first, when you have just added a new skill to their repertoire, you might direct the goal setting. "As I watched your discussions today, I noticed that most members are still forgetting to ask follow-up questions. Turn back to your group and think of three ways your group can remember to include more of those the next time." When you ask each group to report its plan to the rest of the class, you have built in yet another layer of positive interdependence that continues into the next meeting, when members review their plan and execute it in their discussion. Later on, as students become more familiar with the skills necessary for a good meeting, they can begin discussing what skills their particular group needs in order to fine-tune it. For example, our lesson on Table Cards (page 143) teaches students how to do this.

The Bottom Line

We have a clear national mandate to reengineer our classrooms into more friendly, supportive, and productive places.

It's rare in teaching that so many factors coalesce into the kind of opportunity we enjoy today. We have a clear national mandate to reengineer our classrooms into more friendly, supportive, and productive places. We have the research, the knowledge, and the tools to make it happen. If we accept this challenge, we can make even bigger contributions to students' college, career, and community lives. And here's what is really cool: creating a sociable, supportive, hardworking community makes our classroom an even better place to spend an hour, or a day—or a career. What's not to love?

Chapter 3

How to Use This Resource

Overview

There are two parts to this resource. One, which you will grab from the book's companion website (www.corwin.com/teachingsocialskills), is a set of thirty-five projectable skill lessons, ranging from 6 to 25 slides each (468 slides in all, just for the record). Each of these lessons is a classroom-ready slideshow with which you can teach your kids a specific social-academic skill, like being a good partner, asking follow-up questions, or arguing both sides of a controversial topic. While we created these slides in PowerPoint, they are delivered as PDFs, so you can play them on any platform.

Here, in the book, we offer systematic guidance to support you through each lesson. This includes tips, variations, and warnings about any predictable problems for each slide. Thumbnails of the slides adjacent to the step-by-step tips help you keep your place. And, in *italics*, we offer specific teaching language that you can try out, guiding kids through the more complex steps in a lesson.

In our minds' eye, we envision you teaching a lesson with this lay-flat book on your lap (or your desk) and a clicker in the other hand as you advance the slides. By keeping the book open to the corresponding page, you can see what's coming next and quickly spot the guidance we've offered.

So, before teaching a lesson, we suggest that you read through the book's notes, rehearse your teaching a bit, learn of any potential pitfalls, and grab some grace notes. For what it's worth, we think that all school lessons should be offered to kids this way: with oral, written, and illustrated instructions. We already know that projecting instructions is a vital accommodation for language learners and for many kids with IEPs (not to mention our visual/auditory learners). But now we realize that providing lesson instructions in multiple modalities enhances success for *everyone* in the room (including the teacher, who gets useful prompts from the screen).

We envision you teaching a lesson with this lay-flat book on your lap (or your desk) and a clicker in the other hand as you advance the slides.

A Guide to the Slides

Meet the Kids

With the wonderful cartooning skills of our partner Satya Moses, we created a cast of students who represent the lovable range of young people we have worked with over the years. These kids appear in the lessons to illustrate different steps, and to model effective social skills. We hope you enjoy getting to know their distinct personalities, and suspect you'll eventually have a favorite student.

Bri   Jon   Wendy   Avery   Mark   Evelyn   Matt   Lupe

Structure of the Lessons

The *content* of the lessons—the topics discussed, articles read, or controversies addressed—come directly from your subject matter.

Each of the thirty-five slide presentations offers a complete lesson that helps kids learn and practice a particular social-academic subskill. The lessons take from five to forty-five minutes, averaging around twenty. A couple of the more sophisticated ones stretch over two class periods. But these lessons are not time stolen from your curriculum. They don't assign your kids to interact about *nothing*. Instead, the *content* of the lessons—the topics discussed, articles read, or controversies addressed—come directly from your subject matter.

Typically, the lessons begin by posing a problem or need: What are the traits of a good thinking partner? How can we disagree respectfully? What can we do about a dominant "air-hog" in our group? How can we stay focused during long-term research projects? Then, very specific solutions are introduced by the teacher—or co-created with students.

Kids set up and practice each new skill under the teacher's close supervision. When the lesson is done, the students can apply this particular skill as they return to their regular classwork. If you are familiar with the Gradual Release of Responsibility model, you'll recognize what we're up to here. Each lesson moves from a teacher opening, to a shared activity, through guided practice, and on to independence.

The lessons are arranged in a sequence that moves from beginning-the-year activities to deeper levels of collaborative work later on. (More about the teaching order shortly.) Some lessons are designed to be revisited; others may be taught only once. For example, Nancy typically has her students do the five-minute Membership Grid (page 106) *every single day that kids work in small groups, all year long*, reshuffling groups every few weeks to continue building acquaintance, friendliness, and support.

Many of the lessons teach a social skill that, once learned, can be used in later classes without all the introductory steps. For example, Where Do You Stand? is a great structure for discussing any polarizing issue, and kids can jump right into it after the initial lesson has been taught. Others, like Arguing Both Sides, may need to be repeated because the skills involved are very challenging and require repeated practice. And some you will skip, because your kids have already mastered the skill, or it simply isn't a priority right now.

Remember: The minutes spent now are an investment that pays big dividends in classroom climate and student learning all year long.

Order of the Lessons

The lessons are presented in rough chronological order, in seven families:

- Getting Acquainted
- Building Collaboration Skills
- Advanced Partner Work
- Moving Into Small Groups
- Ongoing Discussion Groups
- Arguing Agreeably
- Small-Group Projects

You will probably teach the earlier ones in the opening days of school, and the later ones further down the road. The four to six lessons in each family are also sequential, but most can be taught in a different order—whatever works best for you and your kids.

We designed this resource to support you all year long: thirty-five lessons, or approximately one per week. Since the lessons just take five to forty-five minutes, this should fit into your calendar. Of course, they won't fit neatly into a one-a-week pattern. To begin with, we encourage you to teach the first family of five lessons in the same week, if possible. And as things stretch out after that, you'll find the right sequence and pace for your curriculum and your kids. Finally, as you make time for these lessons, remember that the minutes spent now are an investment that pays big dividends in classroom climate and student learning all year long.

Feel Free to Improvise

You may have good reasons for customizing these lessons to suit your own situation.

It may not be the beginning of the year right now. Sure, first impressions are powerful, and those early days of school inarguably provide a special opportunity to shape kids' social skills and attitudes. But no matter. The best time to start teaching these lessons is *the day you decide that you want your classroom to be more sociable, peaceable, focused, efficient, and fun.* Many teachers have begun these lessons at midyear, after a rough start, with the feeling that their classroom climate needed to be revamped and the kids' social-academic skills directly addressed. Our favorite success stories come from teachers who have turned to these lessons because they were "on the ropes" with a challenging bunch of kids.

Our very general timetable may not fit the kids you have. They may come to you with highly developed social-academic skills and be ready to jump ahead to the later lessons. Or they may arrive completely inexperienced with interactive work and need to spend extra time with the earlier families. Another group of students might appear on your doorstep with surprising gaps or urgent deficiencies that require you to jump around the resource, selecting lessons that fit your kids right now. So we invite you to be very active and practical as you sequence and use these lessons.

You needn't teach every lesson. We think that most kids will benefit from training in all seven families of skills, but they do not need to do every lesson in every family. You will judge how much work your kids need in each area.

You can reteach lessons. In fact, you may *need* to teach some of them more than once for kids to master them. Often, you will do this by substituting a new discussion topic (or article, or subject matter concept), but following the same steps, to reinforce the skill or give kids needed practice.

Create your own lessons. As you teach our lessons, you will quickly recognize that their underlying structures are fairly simple, and that you can use ours as a pattern for developing better ones. When your kids show you a social skills problem or weakness that we haven't covered in this resource, make your own!

The Tips

In addition to the "self-teaching" slides, we also offer several pages of written support for each of the thirty-five lessons. These pages explain why and when to teach the featured lesson, and then provide guidance, suggestions, or support for every slide. Many of these tips are quick and simple (e.g., "be sure to circulate among kids as they practice"), while others offer more complex kinds of support. Some of the lessons require on-the-fly changes, create foreseeable challenges, or offer useful variations. So even though we've done our best to sequence steps for you, you'll still be making plenty of "game time decisions." These are all previewed in the tips. The example on the next page shows how the tips are laid out and how they function.

How the Lessons and Tips Work

Title identifies the name of the social skill or activity being taught.

Why Use It? explains the value of the featured activity.

When to Use It suggests at which time of the year or in the kids' development as collaborators that this lesson best fits.

Preparation notes list what materials you will need and points to consider before teaching the lesson.

LESSON 19: GALLERY WALK

Why Use It?

Gallery Walk is one of our favorite "up and thinking" activities that has kids moving actively around the room, talking and thinking.

As the lesson explains, galleries are places people go to admire and interact with the work of artists and creators. Applied to the classroom, Gallery Walk is one of our favorite "up and thinking" activities that has kids moving actively around the room, talking and thinking about other students' work on a curricular topic. No, they don't go crazy when we let them out of their seats, as long as we have provided the ethic of appreciation and provided careful procedures—just like they do in real art galleries.

When to Use It

This is the go-to structure when kids have created large or graphic work that needs to be shared with many fellow students—or the whole class.

Preparation

- Duplicate copies of an interesting short article, story, or poem. All students will need their own copy.
- Have all the materials ready to go: large poster paper (you may have to go to a primary classroom to get this stuff), colored markers, tape, and pads of sticky notes.
- Think about where in the room (or in the hall) you could create a well-spaced array of posters so small groups can move freely among them.

The Lesson

Slide 1

TITLE: **Gallery Walk**

Slide 2

→ This introduces the culture and purpose of art galleries. You can ask who has been to a museum or art gallery and have volunteers describe the purpose of these institutions.

Slide 3

→ Have kids regard the walls for just a second. They may be blank; they may be festooned with materials.

→ Talk about what it would take to get *this* wall ready to be a gallery.

→ You should already have your own idea about where kids' drawings could be placed; maybe some decorations will need to be temporarily taken down, moved, or covered up. Think about traffic patterns and potential obstacles around the display areas.

Slide 4

→ Trios work best for this activity—having more than three kids trying to write on the same piece of paper, no matter how large, rarely works well.

Slide 5

→ Teach this simple text-coding tool (or another quick annotation strategy of your preference) *before* handing out the article, so kids don't start reading before you have given the instructions.

→ If your students are not familiar with the active-reader mindset of "stop, think, and react," take your time and show them how to leave tracks of their thinking as they read.

Slide-by-Slide Lesson Tips offer step-by-step instructions as well as italicized teaching language that work in tandem with the slides.

Thumbnails of each slide reveal what students will see in each lesson step and help you keep your place.

Assessment and Grading

In general, we do not conduct formal assessments of these short social skill lessons. Instead, we track their "uptake" as we observe kids going about their subsequent work in the curriculum, and especially when they are working with partners or in teams. As we observe, we may just jot running notes or create a simple rubric and carry it on a clipboard as we listen in on student groups or pairs. Such a rubric may be a general one (see Figure 3.1) or one reflecting the core goals of a particular lesson in the resource (Figure 3.2).

Figure 3.1 General Social Skills Observation Rubric

Curriculum Unit:

Date: _____   **Period:** _____   **Time:** _____

Student and Activity	Social Skills Present/Missing	Teacher Action Steps	
		Individual	**Class**
Brad Research Group	• forgot materials	• wrote him a note	
	• not facing partners		• minilesson?
	• couldn't paraphrase		
Rhonda Book Club	• helped Jeff find website		• use as example tomorrow?
	• invited Tonya to talk		
	• summarized Jane's view		

Figure 3.2 Social Skills Lesson Rubric

Lesson: Arguing Both Sides

Date: _____   **Period:** _____   **Time:** _____

Student and Activity	Social Skills Evident/Missing	Action Steps	
		Individual	**Group**
Jessica "dangerous dogs" debate	• worked well with planning partner	• thumbs up	
	• used text evidence		
	• dropped her passionately held view to seek compromise		
Jerry "dangerous dogs" debate	• dominated planning conversation	• coached the group about talk time	• revisit sharing the air lesson?
	• interrupted 3 times		
	• passion high; text evidence thin		

Available for download from **www.corwin.com/teachingsocialskills**

Participation Points

For accountability purposes, we may decide or need to offer points simply for kids fully engaging in our multistep lessons. If you have read our previous work, you know that we favor the use of the "good faith effort" form of grading for such activities. If students show up ready to work and engage fully with others in the lesson, they earn ten points. If they fall short, it's a zero—there are no threes or sevens. This is all-or-nothing grading.

Trouble-Shooting Questions

So I am supposed to be forming student groups of all sizes? What if the numbers don't come out, even for pairs or other size groups?

We do put a lot of stress on specific group sizes—because we want to maximize each kid's airtime and responsibility—and leverage up the positive peer pressure for everyone to join in. The first four families of lessons have kids working with a single partner (different people, but groups of two). When you are just trying to form pairs, there a 50–50 chance things will turn out well. If the number is odd, allow just one group of three—or you can be the partner to the singleton kid. As we move up to fours, it is inevitable that some days the numbers won't work. It is fine to have a couple of groups of three or five. But keep the numbers as close as you can—don't have sixes and twos. In the interest of engagement and accountability, we prefer to solve this problem by going smaller rather than larger.

My kids already know each other well; should I skip the getting-acquainted activities?

We have worked in some rural and private schools where the kids have known each other since birth, and seem to get along well. This is an advantageous starting point, but if you look deeper, everyone doesn't *really* hang out with everyone equally. We also recognize that long-standing animosities can go unaddressed in these groups, and that often teachers don't really press everyone to work together. So no, don't skip the acquaintance-friendliness-support cycle. If kids complain, "But I already know Randy," make a big point that we are learning *new* information about each other, finding out things we don't already know, what makes each of us unique. Also, kids are changing from year to year, having new experiences that alter them profoundly; so we need to keep getting reacquainted with these people who are evolving right in front of us.

I teach in a tough school, where many kids are affiliated with rival gangs. They hate each other. How can this stuff possibly work?

We respect your reality. It may take longer and be more volatile, but a program like this is part of the solution, not the problem. For eight years, Smokey and several colleagues ran a high school in Chicago where many kids were affiliated with black and Hispanic gangs. Outside of school, some bad things happened. But inside, we never had a gang incident, and kids treated each other with friendliness and support—because *the faculty modeled and taught it.* And when civility did break down, we had a peer mediation system that very effectively settled conflicts before they could escalate. Listen: what breaks down hate is knowing people. When we know people as individuals, it gets harder and harder to demonize, discount, or disrespect them.

Are we ready? Let's get sociable!

Part II

Lessons for Building Social-Academic Skills

Chapter 4

Getting Acquainted

Our five opening lessons help you start building your community of engaged and mutually supportive students. These experiences ensure that everyone in the room gets to know each other, not by reputation or past history, but by working directly together, here and now. We rotate partners frequently so everyone has face time with everyone else. Along the way, we ask kids to reflect on these firsthand experiences and name the specific behaviors that make learning with others more fun and interesting.

For highest impact, we suggest you teach these five lessons *in a row, on consecutive days.*

You might use these lessons at the beginning of the school year, or at any time that you've decided to ratchet up the sociability and productivity of your classroom. If your kids already know each other well, stress that we are digging for new information, "things we don't already know about each other." For highest impact, we suggest you teach these five lessons *in a row, on consecutive days.*

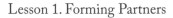

Lesson 1. Forming Partners

Lesson 2. Interviewing Your Partner

Lesson 3. Home Court Advantage

Lesson 4. Friendliness and Support

Lesson 5. Classroom Climate Posters

LESSON 1: FORMING PARTNERS

Why Use It?

Setting your kids up for successful collaboration begins with helping them *manage physical space and their bodies*.

The first, and seemingly the simplest, step in growing a supportive classroom climate is to have kids work with a partner, right? But even this tiniest act of collaboration doesn't automatically work. You've seen it all: kids with five partners, one kid with no partner, pairs facing 180 degrees away from each other, partners talking to other people's partners. It turns out that merely sitting down to work with one other person needs to be explicitly taught and practiced. In short: setting your kids up for successful collaboration begins with helping them *manage physical space and their bodies*.

If you teach younger students, it may feel natural to do this lesson on the rug. If you work with middle or high school kids, you may have to overcome a traditional obstacle to student interaction: rows of desks that seem purposely designed to keep kids apart. And even table seating can keep kids separated unless you set it up right. So, rather than cursing the district's equipment buyers, you'll be teaching the kids how to quietly adjust any kind of furniture for good conversations—and so you can easily move around the room and monitor that student engagement.

When to Use It

Kids need to become comfortable working with many different partners before graduating to larger groups.

Lesson 1 takes only a few minutes and works well on the first day of school—or whenever you decide to introduce social-academic skills to your students. Kids need to become comfortable working with many different partners as they gradually depart the culture of solitary listening toward to one of active participation.

Once students have successfully formed partners, shift into Lesson 2 right away. Observing the interactions as pairs work will show you what social skills kids need next. Since Lessons 1 through 14 are all partner-focused, many opportunities for practice are coming up!

Preparation

- We prefer to partner kids *randomly* (by birthdays, by drawing numbers, or by entering your class list on www.aschool.us/random) as we create the norm: *everyone works with everyone*. Students cannot say "I won't work with him or her."

- Pre-think the student pairings. Count the kids present. If the number is even, everyone will have a partner. If the number is odd, either allow one (but only one) group of three. Or *you* be the leftover kid's partner.

- If you have potentially explosive personal animosities between certain kids in your room, then group them as needed for now. But in the long run, kids who think they don't like one another *must* work together, whether they like it or not, over and over. Acquaintance typically leads to friendliness, which leads to supportive behavior.

The Lesson

Slide 1

TITLE: **Forming Partners**

Slide 2

➔ Project the slide and read aloud.

➔ As students move their desks together, monitor for the desks actually touching.

➔ You want the pairs to be sitting as close together as possible because this move will diminish the opportunity for off-task conversations.

➔ Make it clear that furniture arrangement is nonnegotiable.

➔ Also, remember that kids enjoy their ruts as much as we do. Ruts are boring but predictable and require few risks. If your students are used to working solo, don't be surprised if a few kids complain. One of our favorite reassurances from collaborative learning pioneers Johnson and Johnson is, "You are older and wiser; you can persist longer than the kids can resist." We like to smile and say to the kids, *Humor me for just a few minutes, okay?*

➔ If you have a room where students are sitting at tables instead of desks, go ahead and skip the slide on how to move the desks.

➔ Talk about how to focus solely on one's "shoulder partner," while ignoring the other tablemates—as well as one's friends at the other tables.

➔ Angle the chairs together to help "close out" other students, visually and auditorily.

➔ Be sure to manage the placement of backpacks.

When the kids move desks or chairs, those packs can end up lying right in the middle of the aisle, creating an obstacle course for you, and sooner or later the opportunity to fill out a work related accident report when you twist an ankle. Teach the kids to put *all* their extra stuff on the floor, under the chairs between the partners. This pack-stashing plan will not interfere with the pairs sitting close, but it will keep those snaking straps from ensnaring unwary passersby.

Slide 3

➔ Ask: *What does it mean to introduce yourself to someone you haven't met before? How do you have to introduce yourself to someone new so that you make a good first impression?*

➔ Take a few comments.

➔ Get a volunteer to model with you, how to do introductions. Though the slide depicts a handshake (pretty standard practice in the business world), you might want to substitute what Nancy likes to call "the sanitary fist bump" if the cold and flu season has ensued.

→ Now give partners two minutes to talk.

Slide 4

→ Read this slide aloud and then add a little bit more.

→ *When you treat your partner like a VIP, you will have more fun working together and you will naturally share the work. Also, in a real-job situation, the people who are often laid off first are those who are annoying and can't get along with others. So, when you work with your partner well, you are actually practicing skills that are going to pay off throughout your life!*

Slide 5

→ *As you might have guessed, we just weren't practicing forming partners for the sake of getting a little exercise by dragging the furniture around. We're going to work together with lots of different partners, so here's a preview of the kinds of behaviors good partners engage in.*

→ Read the items from the slide.

→ Now go ahead and segue into another lesson that uses partners.

→ If students are working with their partners for the very first time, we recommend Lesson 2: Interviewing Your Partner, next.

Slide 6

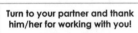

→ Thanking your partner is a motif you'll see repeated throughout most of our lessons. Though some might criticize this as contrived, we believe two things:

- Being thanked for your efforts is always appreciated.

- Kids—or adults—don't often express their thanks; the classroom is the perfect opportunity for students to start living with a mind-set of gratitude.

→ If you share your room with other teachers, be sure to have kids push the furniture back to its "neutral" setting before leaving. If you have a self-contained elementary classroom, lucky you!

Further Comments

If you are a connoisseur of collaboration, you'll recognize that this lesson models what is formally called "shoulder partners"—kids sitting side by side, as opposed to across from each other (which is called "face partners"). Later in the book, when kids are seated in groups of four, each kid can have *two different partners*: the one beside them, and the one facing them. In lessons like Arguing Both Sides, you'll see how we take advantage of this.

We like to begin the year with shoulder partners for a few reasons:

- Whether at a desk or a table, shoulder partners can (and should) sit closer together than face partners, so when all pairs are engaged, the noise level of your classroom will remain lower.

- Shoulder partners are more likely to stay on task since their eye contact is aimed directly at the person next to them. In other seating configurations, students can easily turn to more "not-partners" for "not-the-task" chitchat. In addition to these side conversations interfering with the academic work at hand, they also immediately send this signal to their assigned partner: "I'd much rather work with anyone else than you!"

- Shoulder partners are the foundation of what David Johnson and Roger Johnson (2009) call "face-to-face interaction." After much study, the Johnsons found that the closer you sit with your partner or group—knee to knee, eye to eye—the more likely that group members will stay on task and devote themselves to improving the group's performance. We concur.

LESSON 2: INTERVIEWING YOUR PARTNER

Why Use It?

Students who have good working relationships are far more likely to also be invested in the collaborative academic tasks.

Partner interviewing is one of the most important structures in our skill-building toolkit. When students interview each other, they are enacting the virtuous cycle: *acquaintance leads to friendliness, which leads to supportive behavior.* The more you know about someone, the harder it is to be a bad partner, since you are becoming more personally invested in the relationship. And, students who have good working relationships are far more likely to also be invested in the collaborative academic tasks with which they are presented. Besides the social maintenance benefits of interviewing, this activity offers a nonthreatening platform in which to practice important discussion skills: careful listening, asking follow-up questions, and negotiating topics for discussion.

When to Use It

We made this the second lesson in the book for a reason: the sooner kids begin interviewing each other, the faster your classroom community will grow. We like to use this lesson the first time any pairs work together, and we'll roll kids through several different partners in the following days. As you'll see, the core of this lesson is *teacher modeling*, using a student volunteer as a partner. We carefully show kids *how* to interview a partner before we release them to do it on their own. Later, we also use interviewing as a warm-up every time small groups meet, with lessons like the Membership Grid (page 213 in the Resources and www.corwin.com/teachingsocialskills). Long experience has shown us that even when a group has been working together for a while, members still need brief opportunities to touch base personally, warming up to discussion by getting to know each other just a little bit better each time.

Preparation

- Beforehand, decide how pairs will be formed.
- Decide how students will record their interview notes: on paper you hand out, loose-leaf retrieved from binders, or composition books.
- We like to have students take notes for their first five or six interviews and then use those notes for charting their progress as interviewers. Once students demonstrate skillful listening and questioning, you may choose to eliminate the note taking.

The Lesson

Slide 1

TITLE: **Interviewing Your Partner**

Slide 2

→ Project and read aloud.

Slide 3

→ Project and read aloud.

Slide 4

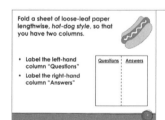

→ Have kids sitting with their partners.

→ With this slide, you're just setting up the note taking. Where we come from, folding a piece of paper vertically is called "hot-dog style," and horizontally is "hamburger" style. Just saying.

Slide 5

→ Ask for one volunteer to be interviewed and a Student Scribe to take notes at the board (you will be the interviewer).

→ If students are reluctant to volunteer, remind them that this class should be a safe place to learn and take risks.

→ When you do get those volunteers, thank them profusely and have the class give each of them a big round of applause.

→ If these volunteers come from two different pairs, match up their now deserted partners as a new working pair. If they were a pair to begin with, no adjustment is needed.

→ Pull two chairs up to the front of the room for the demonstration.

→ Put the chairs in a good partner seating position, as in Lesson 1.

→ Have your interview partner sit down while you set the Student Scribe up at the board or on the computer, using the same two-column format that the students are using.

→ The Scribe's job is to jot down the questions you ask and the information gathered as you conduct your interview.

→ Remind the class:

- *The job of Student Scribe is very hard because it requires one to think and write so quickly. Therefore, do not worry about how the Scribe spells some words. You'll know what the Scribe means, so there's no need to point out any errors.*

Slide 6

→ Have partners brainstorm some school-appropriate interview topics.

→ When they are finished brainstorming, ask pairs to volunteer topic ideas.

→ Let your student partner pick the topic to be interviewed on.

→ Before you begin the interview, remind the observing students:

- *Listen very carefully so that you can offer good follow-up questions that will keep the interview going. I will pause and ask you for ideas as I go. Also, this is an example of the note taking you will need to complete when you conduct your own interviews. So that you will have a good model, be sure to copy down everything that the note taker writes on the board.*

Slide 7

→ Start the interview by asking your student partner to talk a little bit about the chosen topic.

→ Then stop and ask the class: *What information do we have so far?* Give partners thirty seconds to confer.

→ Continue:

- *I want to get more details from my partner. What opened-ended questions could I ask that are based on the details already mentioned? An opened-ended question is one that cannot be answered in a couple of words; your interviewee will really have to do some explaining to answer it.*

→ *Turn back to your partner and brainstorm two or three potential follow-up questions.*

→ Call on a few students and then pick the question that has the most potential.

Slide 8

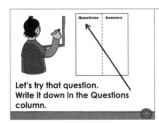

→ While the Student Scribe and the class write down a follow-up in the Questions column, have your partner silently think about it.

→ Tell the class:

- *Having your partner think about the question while you write it down builds in wait time. That way your partner should be able to give you a better, more detailed response.*

Slide 9

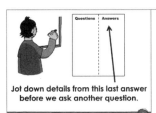

→ After the partner answers, have the note taker and the class jot down some key details in the Answers column.

Slide 10

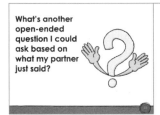

→ Again, ask partners to brainstorm questions based on what information has come out of the interview so far.

→ Pick a question and try it out.

Slide 11

→ The note taking continues for several questions and answers.

→ Conclude your interview after three or four questions and answers.

Slide 12

→ At the end of the interview, allow the note taker and interview subject to return to their partners, thanking them and calling for another big round of applause.

Slide 13

→ Have partners review the interview and talk together about what kinds of questions got the most interesting details.

→ Share responses with the whole class.

Slide 14

→ After sharing, emphasize that the best questions are the ones that show you are really listening and are based on what your partner has just said.

→ Good questions will continue the conversation on a topic in more detail.

→ Also make this clear:

  - *It's the interview subject's job to answer the questions as thoroughly as they can. You're not being a good partner if you are giving one word answers or making it hard for the interview to be conducted.*

Slide 15

→ Check to see if anyone has any questions on how to take notes or conduct the interview.

→ When students are first practicing this interview activity, it's easier if you tell them who interviews first: the person with the darkest color shirt, the person whose birthday is closest to July 4th, etc. Later, students can decide on their own.

→ As students interview, monitor for open-ended questions and good note taking. As the initial interviews are winding down (two to three minutes), call time and have partners switch roles.

Slide 16

→ After partners have experienced both roles (about five to six minutes), end by having a few groups share what they talked about.

Slide 17

→ Then, last but not least, have partners turn to each other and thank each other for the great interviews.

LESSON 3: HOME COURT ADVANTAGE

Why Use It?

In case you haven't noticed, much of TV comedy these days is based on the misfortune of others. And many of the most popular sitcoms create the comedy out of put-downs that friends lob at each other. Unfortunately, our students forget that these friends are not "friends"; they are fictional characters played by actors. No real-life friendship will last very long on a diet of negative feedback. Furthermore, negativity is the message du jour that kids are slamming each other with in the social media world. In this case, the opportunity for anonymity combined with the absence of "face-to-face" interaction provides a powerful recipe for meanness and character assassination. In this often harsh social world, we teachers have to work extra hard to create a different, more empathetic and caring community in our classrooms. That begins with kids dropping their habit of putting down others when they walk through our classroom door.

On social media the opportunity for anonymity combined with the absence of "face-to-face" interaction provides a powerful recipe for meanness and character assassination.

When to Use It

We like to use this lesson at the beginning of the school year if possible, but always before students begin working extensively together, so that they can see how humor at the expense of others is not funny, but hurtful and divisive. Most kids, however they act, deep down do not want to be thought of as mean. Indeed, much of the put-down behavior we see in classrooms is the result of impulsiveness, not meanness. But even an "innocent" put-down often has a harsh and painful effect on the person being put down. This lesson demonstrates why put-downs have no place in the classroom community, and if a student does receive a put-down, it provides a built-in tool for addressing it immediately, versus letting a confrontation escalate.

Preparation

- Decide ahead of time how shoulder partners will pair up.
- Decide how students will record their lists: on paper you hand out, loose-leaf retrieved from their binders, or composition books.

The Lesson

Slide 1

TITLE: **Home Court Advantage**

Slide 2

→ Elaborate a bit on this statistical point:

 ▪ *Teams win more games at home. It doesn't matter whether they are professional or amateur, adult or adolescent, football or basketball.*

→ For further proof, bring in the sports page of your local or school paper and point out the statistics of your own home teams. Of course, if the season isn't over, the final number of wins at home versus away has yet to be determined. If you are doing this lesson at the beginning of the year, the major league baseball stats are pretty robust at this time.

Slide 3

→ Have the predetermined pairs move together quickly.

→ As they work, monitor their progress for time, as well as cajoling the pairs whose lists appear very short.

→ Encourage partners to come up with a list of at least five reasons.

Slide 4

→ Students do not need to recopy their list in the new order. All they need to do is to mark the ranking number next to the reason.

Slide 5

→ Before the sharing and listing commences, designate a Student Scribe so that you will be free to mingle, monitor, and maintain order as the class shares.

→ Call on each pair to make a contribution to the list.

→ Encourage pairs to check off the items on their list that have already been used.

→ When a pair finds that all of their reasons have already been posted, they should share their number one reason.

→ Any time a number one reason is repeated, the Scribe puts a check next to that reason on the board.

→ After going through the pairs, it will usually turn out that the top reasons kids think teams win more games at home are fan support, predictable playing conditions, and high expectations (not wanting to let the fans down).

→ If kids don't think of it, add something like, "Your home fans never boo their own players," or, "You never put down your own players." This sets up the conversation about put-downs coming up.

Slide 6

From now on, this room is our Home Court!

We ARE each other's team members.

And we ARE each other's fans.

→ Once students recognize what helps teams win, turn those reasons back to the classroom.

→ *From now on, this classroom is our Home Court. When we come in every day, we need to remember that we are all on the same team, so we've got to help each other do our very best. At the same time, we are also each other's fans, eager to celebrate each other's successes. From now on, if you feel an urge to shout out a "put-down," think first. Put-downs won't help anyone on this team learn better or do their best.*

→ Home Court helps to eliminate most put-downs, but if a student slips up, smile and ask the kids, "What do we need to remember?" After a while, students will automatically respond to a put-down by saying, "Home Court!" And, don't be surprised if later on in the year you hear it shouted in the hallway as well.

Slide 7

Thank your partner for all the help and support he/she's given you today!

→ You'll see versions of this "thank you" slide in many of the lessons. That's because having students thank each other whenever they work together is so, so important. Over the years, we've found it's one of the most important gestures students can make toward each other that will positively affect the classroom climate. A recent burst of social science research has shown that people who feel and express gratitude are happier and more productive. So:

- Don't let the kids talk you out of it just because they "feel silly." They feel silly or uncomfortable because they aren't used to thanking each other!

- Acknowledge their discomfort and assure them that the more they practice, the easier and more natural thanking each other will be!

LESSON 4: FRIENDLINESS AND SUPPORT

Why Use It?

This lesson extends the job Home Court Advantage begins: creating a community where all students can do their best work because they feel welcomed, appreciated, and supported. As we discussed in Chapter 2, there is little likelihood that every student will enter your room with all of the skills necessary to participate in a high-functioning, high-performance group. The good news is that many skills your students need to interact with each other and your curriculum can be taught explicitly using the same T-Chart lesson format:

1. Make students aware of the skill needed.
2. Brainstorm and make a two-column list of what using that skill would *look like* and *sound like*.
3. Practice using the skill.
4. Reflect on that usage. Celebrate skill successes and make an improvement goal for the next time.

Specifically defining what it means to be friendly and supportive will create a positive tone for your classroom and make behavior expectations clear for all interactions.

When to Use It

Like the other lessons found in this family, we view this one as a collaboration cornerstone. It needs to be taught when students are just starting out with their first partners. Friendliness and Support should closely follow the Home Court lesson. We like to do them both in the same week, and revisit them as necessary until the skills are wired in.

Preparation

- Decide ahead of time how shoulder partners will pair up.
- Decide how students will record their notes: on paper you hand out, loose-leaf retrieved from their binders, or composition books.

The Lesson

Slide 1

TITLE: **Friendliness and Support**

Slide 2

→ Start by having partners turn to their notes on Home Court.

→ You could say:

- *Remember, people can't do their best work when they are afraid others will put them down or make them feel sorry they shared their ideas. I think everyone has been doing a great job using Home Court so far.*

Slide 3

→ In review, you could say:

- *The skill of Friendliness and Support helps people feel at ease, included, and comfortable working with those around them. Without this skill, people have a really hard time working together.*

Slide 4

→ *Take a moment to remember some situations when using this skill was really important. Go ahead and try to recall some events in your own lives where you got this type of treatment, or gave it to someone else, or wished you had been treated this way.*

→ After a minute of silent thinking, have students turn to their partners and talk about all the scenarios they remembered.

→ Allow students to chat for a couple of minutes and then ask:

- *In how many different situations did you find this skill was important? Let's hear what you talked about.*

Slide 5

➔ After students have volunteered their examples of when Friendliness and Support comes in handy, move to this slide and point out any situations depicted here that didn't come up already.

➔ Then you could summarize:

- *Almost any interaction with another person will be more pleasant and beneficial when all parties treat each other with Friendliness and Support.*

Slide 6

➔ *And treating others in this room with Friendliness and Support is something we always want to remember to do!*

Slide 7

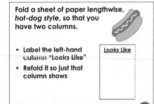

➔ Now it's time for students to work with their partners in making a Skill Chart that defines Friendliness and Support with concrete examples.

➔ Notice that once the columns are created, students should refold the paper in half lengthwise, so that just the left-hand column shows. This will enable them to just focus on one aspect of the skill at a time.

Slide 8

➔ When you show this slide, emphasize that we are just examining the *body language* of groups or pairs who are using the skill of Friendliness and Support.

Slide 9

➔ Before pairs begin to brainstorm, give students one or two examples, such as Eye Contact or Smiling.

- *Focus on positive behaviors. We want to talk about what this skill looks like, not what it doesn't look like. If you think of a negative behavior, try restating it as a positive.*

➔ As pairs brainstorm, monitor and encourage them to keep thinking and writing. If this is the first time your students have ever created a Skill Chart, they might find it difficult because of their unfamiliarity with the task.

➔ After two or three minutes, call students back together.

Slide 10

→ Before the sharing and listing commences, designate a Student Scribe so that you will be free to mingle, monitor, and maintain order as the class shares.

→ As you call on pairs to contribute to the class master list, be sure to record all the behaviors on the board or, ideally, briefly switch from our slides to projectable word processing; that way you'll have a permanent copy of the list.

→ If you do write directly on the board, take a photo of the finished "Looks Like" list with your smartphone before you erase!

→ Instruct students to add all new ideas to their "Looks Like" column so that they have the complete list as well. A typical list will include:

- Eye contact
- Smiling
- Sitting close together
- Focusing on one's partner
- Taking turns speaking
- Nodding in agreement
- Sitting straight, leaning in
- Thumbs up
- Fist bump

Slide 11

→ *Now it's time to talk about what people actually say to each other when they are being friendly and supportive. This time we are creating a list of actual phrases you could use when working with others in the classroom.*

Slide 12

→ Have partners flip their papers over to the right-hand column, label it "Sounds Like." Start by giving a couple of example phrases for everyone to write down:

- "Hi, how are you?"
- "That's a good idea; I didn't think of that."

→ Then give pairs a few minutes to brainstorm friendly, supportive phrases they could say to each other.

→ Monitor the work, encouraging pairs that have finished prematurely.

→ If you notice a pair has written a negatively worded phrase, help them come up with the positive alternative. Instead of "Quit making me do all the work!" replace it with "I need your help and I know you've got some good ideas!"

Slide 13

→ Create a master list of all the positive phrases students could say to each other. Put each phrase in quotes. Remind students to write down all of the new ideas so that their personal lists are just as complete as the one on the board. Typical suggestions often include:

- "Thank you."
- "You're welcome."
- "I appreciate that."
- "Awesome job!"
- "That was smart!"
- "What do you think?"
- "That's interesting."
- "I'd like to hear more about that."

Slide 14

→ Once this list is complete, have students open up their papers so that they are looking at *both* sides of the T-Chart.

→ Now their job is to take turns showering their partners with Friendliness and Support while you walk around the room to see if how they are treating each other matches what Friendliness and Support looks like and sounds like.

→ It is inevitable that a student will blurt out something like, "This is *so* fake!" Admit that it probably does feel that way right now, but if they repeatedly practice Friendliness and Support, it will eventually become a skill they will use smoothly and automatically.

Slide 15

→ Every time students work together, never forget to have them end their meeting by thanking each other. It's surprising what a big difference in classroom community such a small gesture can make!

Further Comments

Never forget that the behaviors behind Home Court and Friendliness and Support are the foundation of *all* collaborative learning. Yes, we know we've only said this at least a half-dozen times already, but this concept is so important it bears repeating. If students do not treat each other well, they will not be successful at working together. Plus, if they are worried about others putting them down and treating them poorly, their academic accomplishments will suffer as well, since no one can put forth her best effort when in a state of fear and discomfort.

A great way to emphasize these skills as you monitor is to pass out stickers (any kind, the sillier the better). When you see or hear students using Home Court and Friendliness and Support skills, give them stickers to put on their notes, handout, or whatever they are working on. Of course, the kids will immediately ask (because they've been conditioned to do so), "Are these worth points?" We always respond by saying, *I don't know; I haven't decided yet. Do you still want a sticker?* To this day, *no one* has ever turned down a sticker. The point is to keep it playful and celebrate kids' new skills.

Also, if you come across a "less than optimal" group, don't ignore it. Stop the members' conversation and say, "I'm not leaving until I hear some Friendliness and Support from each of you. Pick something off the chart and say it to your partner." Make them each take a few turns. It's hard for even the grouchiest group members to stay grouchy after they've said some nice things to each other. And then when they finally crack a smile, hand them some stickers!

Finally, keep in mind that people seldom overtly and positively acknowledge the hard work of others. It will take your continued vigilance and effort to keep revisiting and reminding students to use those Friendliness and Support phrases. Their goal is to get so good at it that they remember to say nice things without your prodding. This takes a lot of practice, but what a pleasant thing to practice.

Never forget that the behaviors behind Home Court and Friendliness and Support are the foundation of *all* collaborative learning.

LESSON 5: CLASSROOM CLIMATE POSTERS

Why Use It?

We make posters because it helps to have a permanent, tangible reminder that students can refer to every day.

Because these skills are the cornerstone of all functioning groups (yeah, we said it again), it helps to have a permanent, tangible reminder that students can refer to every day. Working with a partner to create a poster that advertises one of these skills encourages students to revisit and re-imagine the skill, important steps in making these skills part of one's permanent behavior. Plus, once the posters are up on the walls, they become part of the group forming procedure. Whenever kids get together to work, we always remind them to take a look at the wall and think about how they will make their group Home Court while they treat all their members with Friendliness and Support. And, if a student slips up, all someone has to do is point to the wall!

When to Use It

This lesson is a great follow-up and review after the lessons for Home Court and Friendliness and Support. It's a perfect lesson for Friday, when the kids get a little squirrely. The calming effect of designing and drawing on a piece of butcher paper is impressive. And make sure the posters are up in time for your fall open house. Parents are always pleased to see that you are trying to create an environment where their children are treated in a friendly and respectful manner.

Preparation

- Gather large poster or newsprint paper, skinny colored markers, pencils, pens, and tape for pairs to create their posters.
- Decide ahead of time how students will be forming pairs.
- Students will need to retrieve and refer to their notes on Home Court and Friendliness and Support.

The Lesson

Slide 1

TITLE: **Classroom Climate Posters**

Slide 2

→ *Remember that teams win more games at home than away because of Home Court Advantage. That's the same advantage we want in this classroom. When we work together we are each other's teammates and each other's fans.*

→ *And when we work together we all want to do our best to be friendly and help each other feel respected and appreciated.*

Slide 3

→ Count off the pairs, assigning each pair a number one or two.

→ To avoid confusion, we have the pairs write their assigned number down.

Slide 4

→ Double-check that every pair knows their number with a raise of hands:

- *Number 1 pairs, raise your hands. Good. You're experts on Friendliness and Support.*
- *Now let's see the number 2 pairs. Excellent! You're experts on Home Court Advantage.*

→ Have pairs open up to their notes on Home Court and Friendliness and Support.

→ You might also want to project the class notes on these skills created in earlier lessons.

Slide 5

→ Explain that each pair will be creating a mini-billboard advertisement on their assigned skill.

→ Pass out the newsprint or chart paper (you can cut it in half if needed to fit everyone's posters on the wall) and markers.

→ To begin, have students neatly print their first and last names on the *front* side of their poster in the bottom right-hand corner. Putting their full names on the front side of the poster usually curtails artistic license that may not be entirely school appropriate.

→ We always recommend that students sketch out their designs in pencil before they start coloring.

→ Encourage pairs to proofread each other's lettering as well.

Slide 6

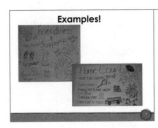

→ Review the criteria. Just project and read this one aloud.

Slide 7

→ Showing students a couple of examples can be helpful in getting them started.

→ It can take students up to thirty minutes to complete their posters, depending on the level of artistry they are going for—and the amount of time you offer.

→ As students finish up, have the tape ready so that they can immediately hang the posters.

Slide 8

→ *Thank your creative partner!*

Slide 9

→ Energetically encourage students to circulate and admire their own work and the posters of others.

Further Comments

Save your best posters from year to year to use as examples for the next class.

Chapter 5

Building Collaboration Skills

Once we have begun to grow a circle of acquaintance and friendliness, we can begin explicitly teaching the ground-level social skills of thinking with a partner. This begins with tasks as simple as managing voice levels, and moves on to creating sequences of questions that dig deeper into each partner's knowledge. By the end of this unit, kids are able to articulate and inventory some key behaviors that help partner work be successful. As these lessons unfold, we keep kids working with different partners, always expanding acquaintance in the room.

By the end of this unit, kids are able to articulate and inventory some key behaviors that help partner work be successful.

LESSON 6: QUIET SIGNAL

Why Use It?

As students begin to work in collaborative groups, they must be able to stop their conversations momentarily so they can receive an additional instruction from you. At the beginning of the year, pulling students back to your attention is relatively easy, since they don't know each other very well. By the end of September, however, it's a different story. Tuned in to Home Court, your classroom community is buzzing with positivity and—sorry to have to tell this—if the pairs and groups are working, the kids would much rather keep talking to each other than break for an interruption from you. That's why an official Quiet Signal is needed. This procedure enables groups to smoothly segue between their lively discussions and the silent focus needed to change gears, hear an instruction, or debrief an activity.

When to Use It

This is another lesson that is best taught early, when students are learning how to function collaboratively. Though it may not be desperately needed the first week of school, establishing this procedure early on will help prevent distractions before they arise.

Preparation

- Decide ahead of time how partners will pair up. This lesson will work best if students have partners with whom they are already acquainted via earlier partner work or interviews.
- When you get to Slide 8, you may want to substitute your own discussion topic.

The Lesson

Slide 1

TITLE: **Quiet Signal**

Slide 2

→ *Throughout the course of the year, you'll be working with a lot of different partners and groups participating in many different activities. That's because the person who talks about the information the most remembers the most. That's why teachers are so smart; we've been talking about our subject for years!*

Slide 3

→ *But to make class run smoothly and also ensure that you get the most out of this class, we'll need a quiet signal. That way you'll hear my directions or your classmate's comments without anyone having to repeat anything.*

Slide 4

→ Just project and read this one aloud.

Slide 5

→ This slide shows some common ways to quickly call a class to attention. There are a lot of different choices to signal students to be quiet:

- Raising one's hand
- Flicking the lights
- Playing a simple chime melody
- Using a whistle
- Clapping rhythmically

→ Our friends at Burley School in Chicago say: "We're coming back in 5 . . . 4 . . . 3 . . . 2 . . . 1 . . . ," thus giving kids several seconds to refocus—and allowing the teacher to speed up or slow down the countdown as needed.

→ You can impose your own preference and simply tell students what signal you will be using. Or, better yet, bring kids in on the decision. Consider the choices mentioned above and any other school-appropriate signals kids want to nominate. Smokey has a handheld sound effects generator that offers very loud choices, including a cavalry charge, car crash, siren, and more. Kids enjoy picking their own favorite quiet signal from among these.

Slide 6

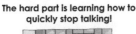

→ *In a moment, you'll have a chance to talk with your partner. Remember, when I give you the quiet signal, you need to quickly stop talking and turn your attention to me. The goal is to move from your conversation to quiet attention in five seconds or less.*

Slide 7

→ Just project and read this one aloud.

Slide 8

→ Substitute another topic if you prefer.

Slide 9

→ Use the quiet signal you chose.

→ As partners break from discussion and reconvene as a class, you can emphasize transition by counting down from five out loud, orally and physically, with your fingers.

→ Emphasize that observing the quiet signal will help the class run smoothly and enable everyone to feel respected and listened to.

Slide 10

→ Reemphasize the importance of being able to move swiftly in and out of groups.

▪ *Class will be the most fun if we can all work together on this!*

Slide 11

→ The less time we waste, the more time we'll have for a great variety of activities.

Further Comments

Sometimes it is hard to regain kids' attention because they are so deeply engaged in the collaborative activity you have set up for them. In these most welcome instances, kids' ignoring the quiet signal might be the greatest compliment you ever got: they are learning so hard they cannot stop!

Other times, if you're still having trouble bringing the class back to attention, explain to the students how their behavior is affecting you:

> *I'm feeling frustrated when it takes us so long to reconvene because I have a lot of interesting activities planned for today, but I don't think we're going to have time for everything. How can we solve this problem together?*

As far as solutions go, we've found that putting the biggest talkers in charge of the quiet signal is often a good way to achieve silence.

Have students brainstorm individually, write their solutions on cards, and turn them in. Then, while the students are engaged in some silent, individual work, read the cards over, pick out the most workable solutions, and then later negotiate a solution with the class. As far as solutions go, we've found that putting the biggest talkers in charge of the quiet signal is often a good way to achieve silence.

As with most skills, being able to move quickly and quietly in and out of discussion is not something most students will master immediately. This behavior really does take a high degree of self-regulation. The quiet signal will need to be practiced consistently in order for it to become a routine response. Also, expect a bit of a breakdown every time you change pairs or groups, so plan to revisit this lesson whenever your classroom mix or seating chart changes.

LESSON 7: USING QUIET VOICES

Why Use It?

It never hurts to teach kids how to speak at a volume suitable for group interaction yet soft enough that it does not disturb nearby groups or adjacent classrooms.

When pairs of kids are working together in a class of thirty or more, that means fifteen students will be talking at the same time. And, when that many people are talking at once, it can get pretty noisy. Now bear in mind, this noisiness seldom interferes with a group's functioning. Today's kids seem really good at tuning out extraneous conversations. Maybe their advanced ignoring skills stem from the ultra-present single earbud wire dangling from ear to device, or maybe it's years of ignoring their parents' exhortations to complete their chores. Nevertheless, the noise of fifteen "loud talkers" may drive *you* crazy and will likely prove distracting to classrooms with which you share a wall or a ceiling. And there are plenty of kids who definitely do have trouble focusing effectively in a cacophonous environment. Therefore, it never hurts to teach kids how to speak at a volume suitable for group interaction yet soft enough that it does not disturb nearby groups or adjacent classrooms.

When to Use It

As your student discussion groups get rolling, monitor the noise level. Typically, the better they get to know each other, the louder they will speak. That noise-level increase is actually positive because it indicates an increased energy level and confidence to speak within the group. The best timing for this lesson is when the groups have reached this "loud" stage of cohesiveness, yet before your next-door neighbor has complained to the principal about your "out-of-control class."

Preparation

- Decide ahead of time how partners will pair up.
- Decide how students will record their notes: on paper you hand out, loose-leaf retrieved from their binders, composition books, or on their tablets.

The Lesson

Slide 1

TITLE: **Using Quiet Voices**

Slide 2

→ The beginning of this lesson is a celebration of skillfulness and high-functioning groups.

Slide 3

→ Just project this one and read aloud.

Slide 4

→ Emphasize that having to solve this problem of talking too loudly is actually a good problem because you've also noticed that the students are engaged and focused on talking with their partners.

Slide 5

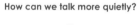

→ This lesson also gives you the chance to touch upon courtesy.

→ Even if your students say they can hear each other just fine, they need to be considerate of others, since the noise will travel to other classrooms that may not want to hear it.

→ And some kids really do find it hard to function amid loud noise.

Slide 6

→ Now it's time for students to work with their partners in making a Skill Chart that defines Using Quiet Voices.

→ Remember to have students refold their papers in half lengthwise so that just the left-hand column shows. This will enable students to just focus on one aspect of the skill at a time.

Slide 7

→ When you show this slide, remember to emphasize that we are just examining the *body language* of groups/pairs who are Speaking Quietly.

Slide 8

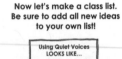

→ Before pairs begin to brainstorm, give students one or two examples, such as Eye Contact or Sitting Close Together.

→ Tell them to focus on positive behaviors. We want to talk about what this skill *looks like*, not what it doesn't look like. (Though reframing negative examples in positive terms can be a source of list items.)

→ As pairs brainstorm, monitor and encourage them to keep thinking and writing. After two or three minutes, give the quiet signal and call students back together.

Slide 9

→ Before the sharing and listing commences, designate a Student Scribe so that you will be free to mingle, monitor, and maintain focus as the class shares.

→ As you call on pairs to contribute to the class master list, be sure to record all the behaviors on the board or, ideally, briefly switch from this slide to projectable word processing; that way you'll have a permanent copy of the list.

→ If you do write directly on the board, take a photo of the finished Looks Like list with your smartphone before you erase. Instruct students to add all new ideas to their Looks Like column so that they have a complete list as well.

→ A typical list will include:

  ▪ Sitting close together

  ▪ Eye contact

  ▪ Leaning toward each other

  ▪ Nodding

  ▪ Smiling

  ▪ Taking notes

  ▪ Finger to lips (quiet signal)

  ▪ Zipper lips (quiet signal)

  ▪ Heads close together

  ▪ One person talking at a time

  ▪ Ignoring other groups

Slide 10

➜ Explain to students that when they brainstorm Sounds Like examples, they are making a list of things people might actually *say* to each other to encourage quiet voices in a group.

Slide 11

➜ Tell students to turn to the right-hand column, label it Sounds Like, and begin to brainstorm possible phrases. Though students will want to include vague descriptors such as "whispering," keep steering the brainstorming toward *actual phrases* they could say as positive reminders to each other to stay quiet. We like to use this example phrase because it emphasizes that quiet voices shouldn't travel beyond the group: *Remember, use your twelve-inch voice.*

➜ Just as before, continue with the same sort of monitoring. Cajole pairs who stop writing after only a couple of phrases.

Slide 12

➜ After a few minutes of brainstorming, create a master list of all the positive phrases students could say to each other.

➜ Put each phrase in quotes or help students figure out how they could turn it into a quote.

➜ If there are a few Sounds Like suggestions that are positive descriptors, yet not actual quotes, it's okay to write them down rather than reject them.

➜ Remind students to copy down all of the new suggestions so that their personal lists are just as complete as the one on the board. Here are some typical items for Sounds Like that students might think of:

- "Remember, use your twelve-inch voice."
- "Move closer so we can talk more quietly."
- "Let's not get too loud."
- "Let's try to talk more quietly."
- "I think other groups can hear us."
- "Nice twelve-inch voice!"
- "I love your quiet enthusiasm."
- "Let's whisper."

Slide 13

➜ Once this list is complete, have students open up their paper so that they are looking at *both* sides of the T-Chart.

➜ Now their job is to start using quiet voices.

➜ Have a topic ready or ask for suggestions; then instruct pairs to interview each other using the skills from Lesson 2 (page 44).

➜ As students talk for about four or five minutes, listen for quiet voices, but also see how well they can maintain a balanced on-topic conversation using their interviewing skills.

Slide 14

➜ Yes, it's broken record time: whenever students work together, never forget to have them end their meeting by thanking each other. It's surprising what a big difference in classroom community such a small gesture can make!

➜ Remind them to listen carefully and use good questions.

LESSON 8: ASKING FOLLOW-UP QUESTIONS

Why Use It?

Though students have had the opportunity to practice listening and asking follow-up questions in a friendly, low-risk interview format, they also need to learn that this same discussion technique is the cornerstone of any purposeful, in-depth academic discussion. Because they already know this interview procedure, we can use the familiar structure to bridge over to content-area discussions.

When to Use It

Fluidly asking follow-up questions during academic discussion is a skill that takes much practice.

This is a lesson we use whenever our groups are beginning to have collaborative discussions on content-area material. It is essential in these conversations that students listen carefully and dig deeply into the ideas of others. Fluidly asking follow-up questions during academic discussion is a skill that takes much practice. We often teach this lesson two or three times—and we return to it whenever we see group discussions jumping too quickly from topic to topic. Discussions can quickly become superficial if members forget to pursue valuable ideas with follow-up questions directed to other group members.

Preparation

- Decide ahead of time how partners will pair up.
- Decide how students will record their lists: on paper you hand out, loose-leaf retrieved from their binders, composition books, or on those beloved iPads.
- For the latter part of this lesson, you will need a *short text* for students to read and create questions about. We recommend nothing longer than a page, and definitely something that relates to your content area and current unit of study. If you choose to photocopy the text, make sure each student has a copy. However, if your text is thought-provoking yet very short, you can simply project it for students to read. Also, we—and the Common Core Standards—consider visual images a form of text, so you could choose a piece of art, a dramatic photograph, a graph, a chart, or some other sort of visual to spur your content-area discussion.

The Lesson

Slide 1

TITLE: **Asking Follow-Up Questions**

Slide 2

→ As we mentioned in the Partner Interview lesson, we consistently use interviews as a low-risk warm-up for academic discussions.

→ Though we teachers often feel pressured to get the academic ball rolling immediately, these five minutes of friendly talk are *always* worth it.

→ Remember, it's much easier to be rude or unhelpful to a stranger than to someone you know, so these warm-up conversations are essential for cementing the climate of Home Court and Friendliness and Support you've been building.

Slide 3

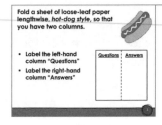

→ Even if you have been using interviewing regularly and slacked off on the formal note taking (which is okay if you think students have mastered good listening and follow-up question skills), do have students set up a page for this interview, since we will return to this note-taking style for the text discussion that begins on Slide 10.

Slide 4

→ Always offer students the opportunity to brainstorm their interview topics.

→ You can have pairs submit ideas on index cards beforehand. Then, whenever it's time for a Partner Interview, you can pull two or three cards and have the class choose from those.

→ We are fine with letting different groups use different topics; there's no reason why every group has to discuss the same subject.

→ Be ready to say how pairs will decide who is interviewed first.

→ If you think some of your kids may be "tough interviews," like some grumpy movie stars, remind them:

  ▪ *It's the interview subject's job to answer the questions as thoroughly as he can. You're not being a good partner if you are making it hard for the interview to be conducted. Remember, this is Home Court.*

Slide 5

→ Just before the interviews begin, review the concept of open-ended questions.

→ Make the distinction between "skinny," short-answer, factual-recall questions ("When is your birthday?") versus broader, deeper, open-ended questions ("How does your family celebrate birthdays?").

➔ Throw one or two short-answer questions out there and ask pairs:

  ▪ *How could you reword this to evoke a longer, more detailed answer?*

➔ Emphasize that the best questions are those that show you are really listening and are directly based on what your partner has just said.

Slide 6

➔ As pairs begin their interviews, observe closely as you monitor.

➔ Don't be afraid to intervene directly.

➔ When you hear a skinny, short-answer question, stop and help the interviewer to rephrase it.

➔ Allow about two or three minutes for the first interviews before asking kids to switch.

Slide 7

➔ Give partners another two or three minutes before reconvening the whole class.

Slide 8

➔ You might have students rate themselves on a scale of 1 to 10 as they consider these questions, and then set a specific improvement goal as well.

Slide 9

➔ Once again, remind students that careful listening and thoughtful follow-up questions are what enable partners to really dig into each other's ideas.

Slide 10

➔ This step assumes that students are familiar with simple annotation. If not, model annotation quickly by reading aloud the first paragraph and showing your annotation. Or, if you are using visual text, project, talk about it out loud, and model your note taking. Then, for the student annotation and interviews, project a new image.

➔ Emphasize that this work is silent. Each partner's goal is to bring as many text-connected ideas as possible to the upcoming conversation.

➔ As students study the material, monitor to make sure everyone is studying and writing notes. For students who finish way before the others, nudge them to reread and see what they can add to their notes.

Slide 11

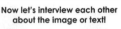

➜ Now students will use the same interview techniques and note taking as they did earlier in the warm-up, except this time they are going to interview their partners about their thoughts connected to the text.

Slide 12

➜ Let each pair decide who will conduct the first interview, but say:

▪ *Make your decision quickly; if you can't decide who's going to start, I'll decide for you.*

➜ As students interview, monitor for asking open-ended questions and good note taking.

➜ Give the interviewers time enough to ask at least three follow-ups, and then call time and have partners switch.

Slide 13

➜ Allow partners to ask several follow-ups before reconvening the class.

Slide 14

➜ Before debriefing the skill of asking follow-up questions, have a few kids share interesting takes on the *topic* of the discussion.

Slide 15

➜ Time to capture the learning from this lesson. As kids offer examples of specific, effective follow-ups, be sure to emphasize the common underlying structures: listening closely and digging deeper.

Slide 16

➜ Thanks, as always!

LESSON 9: THINK-PAIR-SHARE

Why Use It?

Think-pair-share is the number one way to decrease your own teacher talk and decentralize your classroom—one minute at a time.

This is a baseline, bread-and-butter classroom interaction strategy: having kids turn to a partner and talk briefly about a text or topic under study. It is also the most instantaneously transformational structure we can add to our classrooms. Suddenly, it's not just us doing all the thinking, talking, and working; now the kids are taking responsibility and driving the learning, too.

We teachers are so accustomed to telling, lecturing, and presenting that we tend to miss the abundant, nonverbal cues from our audience: the kids aren't getting it, they aren't engaging in it; heck, they aren't even *awake* for it. In our heart of hearts, we know that students don't remember much if all we do is lecture, but the felt need to cover curriculum scares us. But mentioning isn't teaching. Think-pair-share is the number one way to decrease your own teacher talk and decentralize your classroom—one minute at a time.

When to Use It

Just a minute or two, but every day, multiple times a day. Many teachers with whom we work get itchy if they haven't had kids turn and talk for six or seven minutes in a row. Kids need frequent, short opportunities to confirm, clarify, question, synthesize, and consolidate all that good content we teachers are showing and sharing. That means turning and talking four or six or eight times in a class period. If you have five classes, that means twenty to forty times a day. See what we mean by "transformational"?

Preparation

- Copy an interesting, easy, kid-enticing nonfiction article for this. Pick something content-related that helps you advance the curriculum.

The Lesson

Slide 1

TITLE: **Think-Pair-Share**

➔ For this introductory lesson, you'll have kids talk about a short text they will be reading. But in the wide, wide world of school, you can have kids pair-share about anything, anytime: halfway through a lecture, after a science experiment, before or after viewing a film, reflecting on a group project, and more.

Slide 2

➔ Pair kids up, reminding them of the Forming Partners lesson (page 40) as needed.

➔ Be sure to keep mixing kids up with activities like this. The classroom standard is: "Everybody works with everybody regularly," not just your few special friends.

Slide 3

➔ Allow enough time for all kids to finish reading silently and marking the article. If you foresee that students' speed of completion will vary greatly, tell them up front:

▪ *If you finish reading before your partner, go back and see if you can find some more information to annotate.*

➔ There is a bonus reading skill tucked into this collaboration lesson. Kids are practicing a simple form of text annotation—stopping to notice your responses as you read—in three categories. This kind of stop-think-and react strategy is something on which most skilled readers almost invariably rely, whether someone taught it to them or they just invented it for themselves.

Slide 4

➔ Start kids on a series of quick conversations about the three elements for which they annotated.

➔ To keep the pace brisk, give pairs just one minute to share their *interesting* findings from the article.

➔ This lesson actually asks kids to have *three* short conversations with their partner before a whole-class debriefing begins in Slide 7. If you suspect this may be challenging for your kids, you can slow down and have three whole-class debriefings, one after partners discuss each of the three forms of annotation.

Slide 5

➔ Moving on to *important* sections of the text. Keep circulating to support kids who need more direction.

Slide 6

➔ Finally, have pairs talk about any *questions* or curiosities that arose from the reading.

Slide 7

➔ Now start the whole-class debriefing, using the three forms of annotation.

➔ First, ask volunteer pairs to share the most *interesting* information they read or discussed.

Slide 8

➔ Next, move on to hearing pairs report the most *important* information they read or discussed.

Slide 9

➔ Finally, ask the kids to share the *questions* that arose for them during the reading or conversation.

Slide 10

➔ Invite kids to reflect on the value of turning and talking with a partner.

➔ Gratitude to our partners!

LESSON 10: GOOD PARTNER TRAITS

Why Use It?

Unfortunately, when students have a couple of "bad partners" in a row, it makes them reluctant to collaborate because it's frustrating and disappointing.

As students continue to work together, it is important that they begin to recognize *explicitly* why some partnerships click while others fizzle. Without doing thoughtful analysis, students often sum up a bad partner experience with phrases such as "We just didn't get along" or "He/she doesn't like me." Unfortunately, when students have a couple of "bad partners" in a row, it makes them reluctant to collaborate because it's frustrating and disappointing. Also, because students (like most humans) tend to blame others for their misfortunes, they never stop to analyze their own behavior and think about what they could be doing differently when they work with others. This lesson enables students to think about what kinds of partners they want to work with—and what kind of partners they should be!

When to Use It

This lesson works best after students have been working together for a couple of weeks, because their insights will grow out of their recent collaboration experiences in your class. It also comes in handy if you observe kids avoiding or refusing to work with certain other classmates.

Preparation

- Decide ahead of time how partners will pair up.
- You also need to decide how students will record their lists: on paper you hand out, loose-leaf retrieved from their binders, composition books, or Chromebooks, NanoBooks, whatever.

The Lesson

Slide 1

TITLE: **Good Partner Traits**

Slide 2

→ Have pair members turn to each other and talk about what it would be like to work with the partners in Slide 2. Ask:

- *How would that partner's facial expression and body language make you feel?*

- *What would you think the other person thought of you based on their body language?*

- *Which partner do you think would end up doing most of the work?*

→ Give students a minute to discuss and then ask for some volunteers to share reactions.

→ Responses will describe partners who "aren't prepared," "don't care about the work," "are lazy," "aren't nice," "act like the other person is boring/a loser," "won't talk to me."

Slide 3

→ Now have pairs discuss why the body language of these students appears more inviting. Ask:

- *What is it about their facial expressions and body language that might make you feel at ease?*

→ After talking for a minute, volunteers will share things like "smiling," "friendly," "looks prepared," "boy on left looks like he is listening to you," "they all look like they're willing to share the work."

Slide 4

→ Read slide aloud and ask:

- *What behaviors make a work experience pleasant* and *academically productive?*

→ Then give students a minute to chat with a partner and brainstorm some answers.

Slide 5

→ Now have students get out a piece of paper or their spirals/journals and begin brainstorming a list of *all* the behaviors that contribute to working well with a partner.

→ Tell them they should be able to list at least ten different behaviors—minimum!

→ As students consult their partners, monitor the pairs to be sure both kids are writing down ideas. As the listing begins to wane (two to five minutes), reconvene the class.

Slide 6

→ Just project and read instructions aloud.

Slide 7

→ Now it's time to make a master list.

→ Before the sharing and listing commences, designate a Student Scribe so that you will be free to mingle, monitor, and maintain focus as the class shares.

→ Explain that the purpose of the group share is for kids to expand their own lists and add any positive behaviors they didn't happen to think of.

→ Remind partners that if all of their listed items have already been mentioned by the time they have a chance to share, then they can confirm the one behavior they think is most important and the Student Scribe will put a star by that item. Better yet, they should volunteer early and vigorously!

Slide 8

→ Emphasize that you want everyone to have a complete list of class suggestions, not just the ideas from you and your partner.

Slide 9

→ Now it's time for students to do a short, individual reflection. You are asking kids to honestly identify one or two skills to work on, so that their present and future partnerships improve:

  ▪ What behaviors are they really good at?

  ▪ Which ones are weak?

→ Students can write their reflections on the same page as the original list, or you can use index cards as exit slips.

→ If you collect the reflections, be sure to return them the next time that students work together. Before starting the next paired activity, have students review their improvement goals. Then, after this partner work, have them jot down some specific things they said or did that showed they were working toward their goals.

Slide 10

→ Finally, have pairs acknowledge the strengths of their partners by naming the three specific positive behaviors they used when working with each other.

→ And, as always, say thanks!

Chapter 6

Advanced Partner Work

In this family, we move into partner activities that are more complex, take more time, and sometimes involve a series of different partners. Each of these lessons has more steps, more depth, and more challenge for pairs. At this stage, we expect to see students working more fluidly, efficiently, and cheerfully with everyone in the room. The energy generated by meaningful partner work now outweighs kids' reluctance, old cliques, and their mechanical use of social skills.

LESSON 11: ACTIVE LISTENING

Why Use It?

Here's a shocker: most students do not come to us as particularly good listeners. And if we don't fix this promptly, many forms of collaboration will be ruled out of our classrooms. Of course, none of us was born knowing how to give our full attention to another person (except, possibly, to our mothers during our first few months of life). It seems that active listening must always be taught explicitly.

But now, in the world where our students are growing up, focused listening seems to be a dying practice. Who gives their full attention to *anything* anymore? It's so retro; multitasking is the preferred modern mind-set. (We don't know about you, but when we multitask we simply do a crappier job at *everything*.)

Suffice it to say, most of our students need remedial listening. This lesson makes a start of it.

When to Use It

This is an early-in-the-year lesson, for sure. Kids have to get this set of skills down so that they can work effectively with both partners and groups.

This is an early-in-the-year lesson, for sure. Kids have to get this set of skills down so that they can work effectively with both partners and groups. But one practice session may not be enough. If you are not getting the uptake you desire, try doing a fishbowl demonstration with a skillful student or another adult, asking kids to notice what the two of you are doing, and back-mapping those listening behaviors to the ingredients on the Slide 5 list.

Preparation

- Have an interesting, kid-friendly article copied and ready to go. You'll need a copy for each student.

The Lesson

Slide 1

TITLE: Active Listening

→ Sometimes we will open this lesson by saying:

- *Have you ever heard that expression, being "all ears"? What does that mean? Who can share?*

- *By the end of this lesson you probably won't actually grow any more ears, but the ones you already have might get a little bigger.*

Slide 2

→ *What positive body language do you notice?*

Slide 3

→ Take ideas from a few volunteers as you ask:

- *What do you notice kids doing in these two pictures? Even without hearing any audio, we can infer that these kids are practicing active listening. So let's try it ourselves now.*

Slide 4

→ Pass out the article. As they read silently, kids will be using the simplest text annotation model of all—when you notice something that would be fun to talk about with your partner, you stop and mark or underline it.

→ Later, pairs can refer back to this section to start or sustain a conversation.

Slide 5

→ Here we show the most commonly cited ingredients of active listening.

→ Go through them patiently, making sure kids understand what each one means.

→ If your students think of new items, cheer their thinking and add them to the list!

→ Explain that when the demonstration starts, they should try to use as many of these behaviors as they can.

Slide 6

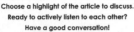

Choose a highlight of the article to discuss.
Ready to actively listen to each other?
Have a good conversation!

I will leave the rules of active listening up on the screen to remind you.

→ Be emphatic and explicit about these steps:

- Review your notes
- Together with your partner, pick a topic

→ When you are confident that kids understand the task, skip right ahead to Slide 7, so they will have the rules in front of them as they experiment.

Slide 7

Rules of ACTIVE Listening
To show the speaker you are listening:

- Turn your body or lean toward the speaker.
- Maintain eye contact with the speaker.
- Nod and encourage with words like *uh-huh*.
- Look and act interested.
- Ask questions to get more information.
- When appropriate, jot down brief notes.
- Be ready to summarize what the speaker said.

→ Keep the rules visible to support kids' practice.

Slide 8

Get ready to summarize your partner's comments right back to him/her.

Take a minute to think.

Put your partner's main ideas into your own words and be as accurate as you can.

Ready?

Summarize!

→ *Now we are narrowing in on one vital and challenging aspect of active listening: paraphrasing what your partner said. This really requires attention and focus—if you are just thoughtlessly nodding while your partner speaks (and mainly waiting for your next turn to come), you'll be unable to summarize.*

→ Allow kids the think time to recollect and create a gist statement of what their partner said. Encourage them to jot down notes if that is helpful.

→ Let the partner with the earliest birthday try it out.

Slide 9

Partners, was the summary accurate?
How could it be even better?

Now switch roles and summarize.

Then, talk about how it went.

→ In their pairs, have the kids debrief the process.

→ Challenge them to find ways of making the next summary even more accurate when they switch partners.

→ Now signal partner #2 to give his or her summary.

Slide 10

Let's hear what some partners had to say about the article. Will someone volunteer?

Before our volunteer shares with us, let's get ready to listen actively.

How are we going to show that we are engaged and attentive?

Remind us.

→ Now you shift to whole-class talk, where kids will continue to practice the same active listening habits, just in a larger group setting.

→ Set this up by first getting one kid to volunteer to share with the class—but then putting that student "on hold" for a minute while you discuss active listening with the audience members.

→ After kids have offered their own reminders for active listening, show the next slide.

Slide 11

EVERYONE...

- Turn your body toward the speaker.
- Maintain eye contact.
- Nod and encourage with words like *uh-huh*.
- Look and act interested.
- Jot down brief notes.
- Ask questions to get more information.
- Be ready to summarize what the speaker said.

→ This is basically the earlier active listening ingredients list (with a few tweaks to better represent large groups).

→ Kids should be ready to hear the volunteer's report, using their best active listening skills.

Slide 12

→ Now invite your volunteer to share.

Slide 13

→ When the volunteer is finished, get someone to start summarizing.

→ Invite other kids to join in and improve it.

→ Keep asking the volunteer if the summaries are accurate, and seek more students to clarify, refine, and improve the summary.

Additional Suggestion

• Using the list from Slide 11, have kids reflect on their success in using the other ingredients of active listening.

Further Comments

Slide 14

Active Listening is something kids will depend on—and something that requires plenty of practice. You can redo this lesson with different partners and topics. You can do shorter, more targeted minilessons on other active listening "subskills," such as body language, supportive language, or asking questions.

LESSON 12: EXTENDING CONVERSATION

Why Use It?

As students become more accustomed to working together, we want them to start taking more control over their own conversations.

As students become more accustomed to working together, we want them to start taking more control over their own conversations. The Neighborhood Map is a great tool when pairs are practicing ways of beginning and extending conversations. Plus, the map is an absolute treasure chest of personal writing prompts.

Students start by drawing a map of a neighborhood where they have lived, adding symbols that represent their memories. These maps typically evoke lots of thought and creativity. When other students look at them, they have a hard time deciding which memory they want to hear about. As students continue to use their maps for conversation, they automatically add and revise the maps because sharing gives them new ideas and helps them recall memories they did not initially include. Sometimes, sharing memories from one map even spurs students to create new maps, with different neighborhoods and different memories. Go for it!

Another good reason for making a Neighborhood Map is that it creates detailed notes that use few words. For English language learners, graphic note taking is a perfect accommodation. Pictures transcend language. When students draw their maps, they are also mentally rehearsing their stories. While it is sometimes hard for language learners to respond quickly in an impromptu conversation, this mental rehearsal enables them to share their stories with greater confidence.

When to Use It

Extending conversation via the Neighborhood Map is something that can be started anytime. However, students find it fun to begin their maps early in the year. After the initial conversations, the maps can be put away and then retrieved periodically for revision and new conversation, possibly when the class mix changes or students have new partners and new groups. As you'll see, we use the maps again in Lesson 13.

Preparation

- Gather plain paper (legal size is better), skinny colored markers, colored pencils, plain pencils, or pens.
- Decide how students will be forming pairs in Slide 7, when it comes time to exchange and talk about their maps.

The Lesson

Slide 1

TITLE: **Extending Conversation**

Slide 2

→ When introducing this assignment, we really emphasize that kids need to think of a place that holds a lot of memories.

→ This could include some of the examples pictured here or someplace else: the elementary school, a sports field, the woods, a place of work (if students are older), etc.

Slide 3

→ Overview of map making, with one student example.

→ *It might look something like this.*

Slide 4

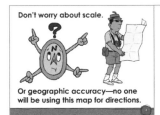

→ *As you think about your map, don't worry about accuracy or directions or scale. This is not a map anyone is going to try to use to find a physical location. This map is the exact opposite of getting directions from Google Maps!*

Slide 5

→ *What is important about this map is the memories. Also, as you think about your neighborhood and events that happened there, keep in mind that your maps will be shared with others. If there is a memory that's too personal to share, you probably don't want to include it on your map.*

→ Yes, we are asking that students censor what they might write down, but the whole point of this activity is to create an inventory of ideas that *can* be shared. Later, when we start to use these maps with partners, we've found it very frustrating for kids when their partners refuse to share anything on their maps because it is "too personal"; hence, the sharable memory rule.

→ If you are working with older kids, you will also want to remind them:

   ▪ *As your map begins to take shape in your thinking, remember that we've got to stick to school-appropriate memories.*

Slide 6

→ Redisplay the example map and answer any questions.

→ You'll want to decide on a minimum number of memories for the map, possibly ten to begin with. Now give students some time to sketch. With plenty of drawing time, it's not uncommon for kids to label twenty-five memories, events, and highlights.

→ You might get the kids started by having them think about questions like these:

- *What did your yard or your street look like? What events happened there?*

- *Whom did you hang around with in your neighborhood as you were growing up? Where did you like to hang out?*

- *What games or sports did you play in your neighborhood? Where?*

- *Ever have an accident or injury? Ever get in trouble?*

- *Did you have any pets? Which ones stand out? What stories could you tell about them?*

- *What was your first day of school like when you entered elementary school? Middle school? High school?*

- *What's in your bedroom that holds memories? What souvenirs, trophies, sports items, or clothing do you keep because of the memory?*

- *What memories involve your siblings?*

→ We like to use ten to fifteen minutes in class to get a start on the maps and then stop to share what they've gotten so far. If you choose, students can continue to work on their maps outside of class—or they can move right on to the next step.

→ As students sketch, monitor closely, zooming in on those who finish super-early. For those students, use some quick conferencing to help them think of more memories for the map.

→ Be sure to decide ahead of time how "final draft" you want these maps to be. We often just treat them as ongoing rough sketches that, as we mentioned earlier, are added to as the year progresses. However, students often enjoy creating a neat, colorful, and carefully planned final version. This might be something to do toward the end of the year, when all possible memories are recorded on the rough drafts.

Slide 7

→ Monitor students once they exchange maps and study them. For those who only give their map a cursory glance, ask them about the memory they've chosen and what questions they plan to ask.

→ If you desire, have students jot down the memory that's sparked curiosity; then, underneath, have them list questions they could ask when they interview their partner about that memory.

Slide 8

→ Let partners decide who will start.

→ Before the interviews begin, review how the best follow-up questions result from careful listening.

→ Remind those being interviewed to give plenty of interesting details.

Slide 9

→ Allow about two minutes per pairing.

Slide 10

→ Hearing a few stories is a great way to introduce the concept of *segue*. Rather than just hearing some memories at random, challenge students to find ways to connect the next story with the previous one.

  ▪ *What do they have in common?*

Slide 11

→ *Never forget saying thank you!*

→ It doesn't take much time, and the contribution it makes to a positive environment is truly astounding. If students ever complain that it seems phony, just tell them that they need more practice at thanking others. Eventually, it will be a skill that comes naturally and seems real. Also, being thanked for one's efforts is something people never get tired of!

LESSON 13: EXPANDING ACQUAINTANCE WITH AN APPOINTMENT CLOCK

Why Use It?

The more familiar students become with predictable procedures, the less overt direction they need from you.

Once students can have sustained conversations with a few partners, it's time for them to shift around, having short "appointments" with multiple members of the class. This ensures that everybody has a chance to work with everyone else, solidifying classroom friendships. While the appointments are brief, these quick, positive interactions yield ample rewards later on, when you shuffle groups and students have to connect with new members. Think how much smoother group changes will be when students meet their new members and think, "I had a lot of fun talking to her when we did the Appointment Clock!"

Also, remember those Neighborhood Maps from Lesson 12? We're giving them some mileage in this lesson as well. By this time, you've probably noticed that, whenever possible, we try to reuse routines and procedures with which your students are already familiar. This helps you save time in your instructions because everything isn't always "new." Also, the more familiar students become with predictable procedures, the less overt direction they need from you.

When to Use It

We always recommend that you go a few weeks into the school year before using lessons that require all of your students to be out of their seats. For proper monitoring, corralling misbehavior, and fishing shy students out of your room's hidden corners, you've really got to know everybody's names. But once that is accomplished, we find that students grow to enjoy these active lessons because all the sitting they do every day can grow pretty tedious.

Preparation

- Photocopy the Appointment Clock (see page 212 in the Resources and www.corwin.com/teachingsocialskills) for each class member.
- Each student will need their Neighborhood Map from the Extending Conversation lesson.

The Lesson

TITLE: **Expanding Acquaintance With an Appointment Clock**

➜ Project and read aloud.

➜ Project and read aloud.

➜ Monitor to make sure everyone has written their names down before the next slide.

➜ *Today, you're going to have the opportunity to work with some different class members. Your primary goal is to meet new people, so do your best not to make appointments with your current partner or your old friends. Any questions?*

➜ *Before finding your first partner, wait for the next instruction.*

➜ *Everybody stand up. We're going to start with 1:00.*

➜ *When I say go! find someone who has the same eye color as you. Try your best not to pair up with an old partner or friend. Remember, your goal is to meet new people, classmates you have yet to work with.*

Slide 7

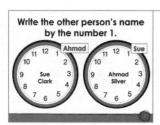

→ *When you find your "eye color" appointment, write each other's names down by 1:00; then double-check that you've written each other's names down under the same time. Believe me, it's easy to make a mistake.*

→ As students look for partners, circulate and intervene when necessary. If you see a huddle of friends converging, head them off. If you see a wallflower fading, pull him back into the mix.

→ If you have an odd number of students, have *everyone* write down the extra person's name by the appointment number and star it; this indicates that this student will act as a substitute for that number on the clock. Sooner or later, someone's partner will be absent and that person can be the substitute appointment. When this "substitute" procedure is used, be sure to announce:

  ▪ *Since we have an odd number of students today, we will need a* different *student to volunteer as a substitute for each appointment hour.*

Slide 8

→ *This time it's 2:00. Find someone who has a different hair color than you. Remember, your goal is to meet* new *people, classmates you have yet to work with. When you find your "hair color" appointment, write each other's names down by 2:00; then double-check that you've written each other's names down under the same time.*

→ If necessary, also remind students:

  ▪ *Don't forget we will need someone new to volunteer to be a 2:00 substitute.*

Slide 9

→ Project and read aloud.

→ If necessary, also remind students:

  ▪ *Don't forget we will need someone new to volunteer to be a 3:00 substitute.*

Slide 10

→ Project and read aloud.

→ If necessary, also remind students:

  ▪ *Don't forget we will need someone new to volunteer to be a 4:00 substitute.*

Slide 11

→ Project and read aloud.

Slide 12

→ Project and read aloud.

→ Call out one of the appointment numbers (1 to 4).

→ Wait for students to find the correct partners. If you have an uneven number of students and there are no "substitute vacancies," the designated substitute can join the pair of her choice.

Slide 13

→ Project and read aloud.

→ Having already completed the original Extending Conversation lesson, students should be familiar with conducting memoir interviews based on trading their Neighborhood Maps.

→ Give appointment pairs a minute to study each other's maps and then get the interviews started. Give each partner two to three minutes for their interview. Remember to call time when partners need to switch roles and begin the second interview.

Slide 14

→ You can end the lesson here or go on to Slide 15.

→ Yes, we know we sound like a broken record (or is it a broken iPhone Cloud?), but the more you can have your students thank one another, the better the classroom climate will be!

Slide 15

→ Call out a new appointment time and conduct another round of memoir interviews.

→ You may return to Slides 12, 13, and 14, or stay on Slide 15 and just repeat the directions orally as you monitor the appointment meetings.

→ We generally recommend meeting only a couple of appointments on any given day. Or, if you're short on time, feel free to stretch these four appointments out over three more days. When you are done, make sure your students safely stow away their maps and Appointment Clocks for future retrieval and use.

Further Comments

Adding Appointments

After completing their first four meetings, students will understand the Appointment Clock procedure. Depending on your class, you can just set students loose to make their own additional appointments or continue to structure them in the way that we did. But to make it more fun, have the kids think up the new appointment categories. Also, on subsequent days, only look for one or two partners at a time, and then be sure to budget the time so that students can revisit each new appointment for a quick memoir interview. Finally, there's no rule that says students have to make twelve new appointments. This activity is flexible, so tailor it to your needs.

Reconnecting With Previous Appointments

Though we demonstrate Appointment Clock meetings using the Neighborhood Map, students can get together and discuss *any topic*. A fun, quick discussion alternative is reading choices from one of the many *Would You Rather . . .* books available and having appointments explain to each other which choice they would make and why. Just type this book title into Amazon and you will see quite an assortment from which to choose; we recommend sticking with the books geared toward children. Many of the books for adults have some good topics that could be used in the classroom, but they also have whole chapters that would be completely unsuitable.

Appointment Clocks can also be used to share SSR books or review information. Encourage your students to think of new ways for them to productively meet with their appointments.

This lesson dramatically shows how many different "soft skills" people need in order to successfully meet and converse with a variety of partners.

Highlighting Soft Skills

This lesson dramatically shows how many different "soft skills" people need in order to successfully meet and converse with a variety of partners. Maybe not after the first meeting, but after a few appointments, take the time to discuss this. Here are the skills students might list:

- Learning and remembering names
- Making people comfortable using Friendliness and Support
- Listening carefully
- Asking open-ended questions
- Speaking quietly
- Using positive body language
- Staying on task
- Focusing on their partner

Guess what? These are the same skills that come in handy in a job interview!

LESSON 14: MINGLE JIGSAW

Why Use It?

As with our other mingling lessons, we think it is very useful for kids to make their thinking concrete with physical activity. We sometimes forget how completely unnatural motionless listening is to the energetic middle-high organism.

When to Use It

This is a very useful activity to kids when they are starting off on a new topic or reading a new text, and they need to activate their background knowledge and build curiosity about the subject. The fact that they are up and thinking, mingling through the room in a game-like, jigsawing quest—with a "right answer" waiting at the end—makes kids want to buy in.

Preparation

- Pass out 3 × 5 cards to students for note taking on an interest they have.

The Lesson

Slide 1

TITLE: **Mingle Jigsaw**

→ Just invite kids to talk about what the word *mingle* means, or some occasions where people mingle.

Slide 2

→ Ask a few volunteers to share mingling experiences.

→ The key attribute of mingling is that you seek out short conversations with lots of people at an event.

Slide 3

→ A visual preview of the process.

Slide 4

→ Tell kids that, if possible, you want them to share some new, fresh information about themselves.

→ The first time we have kids mingle, we use their personal interests as the topic. But later, mingles can be academic. Students can have the same kind of short conversations about a subject-area article concept, or controversy. When picking such a topic, be sure that it is really discussable, and that kids have plenty of time to collect their thoughts before mingling.

Slide 5

→ Allow about a minute for note writing.

Slide 6

→ Know what space you will use for kids to mingle—and have it cleared beforehand. Or have kids move furniture as needed now.

→ You really need an open space for partners to meet up; once paired, they can step off into the edges of the room.

Slide 7

→ You may want to model this yourself with a student, turning to stand together in a good talking position. Demonstrate how you'd step off the dance floor to talk, and then come back when the minute is up.

→ Model how a pair would come back to the dance floor, thank each other, and wave cards to find a new partner.

Slide 8

→ It's important to stress how fast the mingle moves.

Slide 9

→ Reiterate the procedure.

Slide 10

→ Circulate actively, calling out time at one-minute intervals.

→ The first time kids do this, they will really need your coaching to finish the conversation and find new partners—so don't be shy.

→ Don't worry about the eight partners goal. The number of pairings will vary based on how interest people get in their partners. Call time after ten minutes or when interaction starts to fade.

Slide 11

→ This is a good time to practice the class's Quiet Signal.

→ Give kids a minute to settle.

Slide 12

→ Help students practice active listening by getting several volunteers to share *what one of their partners shared.*

Slide 13

➜ Let partners add on, embellish, or fact-check.

Slide 14

➜ Thanks all around.

Chapter 7

Moving Into Small Groups

Next, students bring the interaction "moves" they've honed with partners into working with larger groups—usually four members, and rarely more. We expect kids to bring along all the skills they have developed with partners, and now, to add some more. We first loop back to acquaintance building through interviewing, to transfer that friendly, supportive attitude to working with more partners. Then, the next four lessons offer practice in basic group work; all these structures are curriculum-friendly, and can be used with content from any subject area.

Lesson 15. Group Membership Grid Interviews

Lesson 16. Sharing the Air

Lesson 17. Saving the Last Word

Lesson 18. Write-Arounds

Lesson 19. Gallery Walk

LESSON 15: GROUP MEMBERSHIP GRID INTERVIEWS

Why Use It?

Just as partner interviews served as a warm-up before pairs commenced academic discussion, the same holds true for larger groups. Membership Grid interviews take just five minutes of class time, but they pay off big-time in the work that follows. Starting with a kid-friendly discussion topic results in better content-area discussions, because asking good follow-up questions is the essence of the "warm-up" itself.

When to Use It

We try to use the Membership Grid whenever larger groups meet.

We try to use the Membership Grid whenever larger groups (usually four members) meet. The few minutes spent talking about a kid-chosen "recreational" topic sets the stage for the rest of the subject-matter meeting. We have found that in our mania for "time on task," pushing groups immediately into complex content often results in discussions that may be neither energetic nor rich. That's because you have to be interested in your members in order to be interested in their ideas. The Membership Grid activity makes members much more interesting to one another. Don't be tempted to save some time and skip this step when groups meet.

Preparation

- Decide ahead of time how students will form longer-standing work groups of three to five. We don't recommend using groups larger than four (or five, if you have some students that are often absent).

- Make sure students know how you want them to move the furniture and sit so that their focus will be on the group. Since students may be working in the same groups for a week or more, you might want to recalibrate the seating chart to accommodate expedient group formation.

- Decide how students will record their group's interview topic list: on paper you hand out, or loose-leaf retrieved from their binders, composition books, or on tablet computers.

- Each student will need a copy of the Membership Grid handout (page 213 in the Resources and www.corwin.com/teachingsocialskills).

The Lesson

Slide 1

TITLE: **Group Membership Grid Interviews**

Slide 2

→ Once the groups are together, have them brainstorm some good, school-appropriate interview topics. Since students will already be very familiar with partner interviews, they should be ready to provide some good choices.

→ Allow three to five minutes of brainstorming time.

Slide 3

→ Take some suggestions and then pick one that will work for everyone.

→ Tell the groups to save their leftover ideas because they will get to use them later.

→ If anyone groans at the topic choice, give the class some pointers about how they could be interviewed on the topic. For example, if the topic is pets and you don't have any pets, the group could still interview you on why you don't have pets or what pets you'd like to have some day.

Slide 4

→ Pass out the Membership Grid forms and show students how to fill them out.

→ In the boxes for group members' names, kids should fill in the other students' names, *but not their own,* since they won't be taking notes when they are the subject of the interview.

→ That means if there are four people in a group, there will be three name boxes filled in; if there are five people in a group, all four name boxes will be filled in.

→ Since you only use one row per meeting, this form can be used for five different meetings. You may wish to remind students that you will be collecting the filled-out forms periodically to assess their improving interview skills.

Slide 5

→ Show students the example.

→ The idea is not to transcribe every word an interviewee says, but to jot down only key words and phrases that really capture the essence of the comments.

→ Point out that they will have to write small, so that all the information stays inside the proper box.

→ Now ask kids what's missing in the example:

- First, the date is absent from the Topic box.

- Second, it looks like the group could have done a better job asking open-ended questions; some of the answer boxes look pretty skimpy in the specific detail department. Talk about what questions the members could have asked to get beyond those superficial answers. For example, the group could have asked Lisa, "What happened in the movie that was gross?"

Slide 6

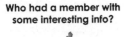

Conducting the Interview

1. Interview one member at a time.
2. All other members participate in the interview by listening and asking questions.
3. Everyone records answer details on their Membership Grids.
4. After about a minute, interview someone else.
5. Continue until everyone in your group has been interviewed.

→ Project and read the directions aloud.

→ Be sure to emphasize that one person gets interviewed at a time, but all other members help conduct the interview.

- That means *everyone* is responsible for asking open-ended follow-up questions as each member is interviewed.

- *Everyone* should be jotting down interesting answers as they emerge; members don't just write down the answer to the question they asked.

→ Monitor the groups or even sit in briefly to make sure everyone is following the directions and taking an active role in the interviewing.

Slide 7

Who had a member with some interesting info?

→ Invite groups to share some interesting information that arose.

Slide 8

What open-ended questions helped to keep the interviews going?

→ Follow up by asking the groups who shared to recall the open-ended questions that made the interview so fascinating.

Slide 9

Thank your group members for the great interview questions and interesting conversation.

→ No meeting is complete unless it is celebrated with a thank you!

LESSON 16: SHARING THE AIR

Why Use It?

Our model of collaboration mostly calls for "leaderless" groups—meaning teams where *every member shares equally* in the work, not taking turns watching the latest "boss" do everything. One phenomenon that can undermine this even-steven distribution is when one person consistently dominates the meetings (this happens with grownups, too). Sometimes that person is trying to be helpful by carrying the load for members who are shy, sleepy, uninvolved, or just plain slacking off. Other times, these air-hogs are simply just in love with the sound of their own voices and are drowning out other potential participants.

When to Use It

Unbalanced airtime can be a recurrent problem; as long as some students have big egos, and others are happy to sit quietly by, we have to keep revisiting this lesson.

There are two logical times when this lesson is needed. Initially, you'll introduce it when kids move from pairs to larger group work. And then you may revisit it anytime you notice air-hogging or slacking occurring among your students. If the issue is plaguing just one group, you can just step in and coach those kids. But if asymmetrical participation is more widespread, you will want to do a whole-class lesson the next day. Unbalanced airtime in groups can be a recurrent problem; as long as some students have big egos, and others are happy to sit quietly by, we have to keep revisiting this lesson. If we don't, then responsibility, action, and accountability aren't being required of everyone.

Preparation

- At Slide 9, you'll need a discussion topic for the kids. You can use a very short nonfiction article related to your subject. Even better, choose a quotation, chart, or puzzle that can be projected—no handouts required, no trees die. Just be sure the material you select will engage kids for three to five minutes of discussion.

The Lesson

Slide 1

TITLE: **Sharing the Air**

Slide 2

→ Just project and read this one aloud.

Slide 3

→ You could ask:
  - *Has anyone ever been in a discussion like that? Were you the hog or the log?*

Slide 4

→ Give groups about three minutes to think and jot.

→ When there is one minute left, remind them that they will need to share their list of five possible solutions.

Slide 5

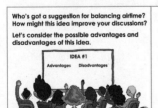

→ Take one suggestion from several groups, ideally one from every group.

→ Write these on the board or chart paper so they can be referred to later.

→ Be sure to spend time on the potential disadvantages of each suggestion. For example: often, kids' first idea is to use a timer or watch. While this exercise can be informative, it does not lead to authentic conversations, which are characterized by spontaneous give and take, and responses of varying lengths.

→ Another likely suggestion (which we do find useful, for a brief training period) is using "talk tokens" or a "talking stick" to meter out each person's talk time. In our version of this, each group member gets five poker chips. Every time you speak, you have to spend a chip. When you are out of chips, you have to shut up and the remaining kids have to pick up the conversation until all chips are spent. Then everyone goes back to the bank for another five chips, and the discussion continues. Again, this approach has the disadvantage of being somewhat mechanical, but the dramatic feedback it provides to air-hogs often works where verbal guidance is ineffective.

Slide 6

→ Take your time to thoroughly process several students' suggestions. You are building buy-in here.

Slide 7

→ One more suggestion.

Slide 8

→ By all means, let the listing continue to six or ten good ideas, if the kids keep generating them.

→ Feel free to add your own entry here if a key option is missing from the list.

Slide 9

→ Now you are preparing the kids to choose one strategy for balancing airtime and try it out.

→ But first, they need a topic for discussion.

→ Hand out or project the material you have chosen and give students some time to think it over and make pre-discussion notes.

→ If kids struggle with the writing, you can suggest:

- *Write down three things about this (article, quote, topic) that you'd like to talk about with your groups.*

Slide 10

→ Now let groups choose one strategy from the list you co-created earlier, circle up, and try it out on the topic they've chosen.

Slide 11

→ Give kids three to five minutes of discussion time, depending on the engagement level.

→ Listen into groups to collect some examples or observations you can share later.

Slide 12

➜ First debrief the *content* of the conversation—what kids had to say about the topic, article, or quotation you provided.

Slide 13

➜ Now invite conversation about the *process* of the discussion, especially about how the chosen airtime-spreading strategy worked out.

➜ Try to identify the approaches that led to the greatest success, and highlight these on the list.

➜ If there were ideas that bombed universally, you can dramatically cross them out.

Slide 14

➜ *Great sharing!*

LESSON 17: SAVING THE LAST WORD

Why Use It?

Many times the student with the great question just surges ahead and answers it before anyone else gets a shot.

Even when students get better at bringing really interesting discussion questions to group meetings, the resulting conversations can still fall flat. We think: How can this be? That kid had a great question! Why didn't anything happen? The kids talked about it for two seconds and then moved on! After years of observation, we've diagnosed the problem. Many times the student with the great question just surges ahead and answers it before anyone else gets a shot. And when the person who asked the question answers the question, what is the point of saying anything? If anyone knows the answer, it's got to be the person who wrote the question, right? End of discussion.

So we solve this problem by breaking discussions down into a series of steps that require everyone else in the group to weigh in before the person we call the discussion starter. Instead of quickly answering her own question, the discussion starter can only pose it and then announce, "Save the last word for me!"

When to Use It

Use this lesson when you want students to share their ideas more evenly in the group, and are reaching toward more extended discussion. Meant for groups of three or four, this lesson works best when groups have worked together in discussion a couple of times.

Preparation

- Decide ahead of time how students will form ongoing work groups of three to five.

- Members will need to come to their group meeting with an assigned piece of content-area text read and annotated for discussion; all students will be reading and annotating the same piece. Depending on time, the reading and annotation may be completed in class or for homework. However, if you can fit the reading into the class period, it will guarantee that everyone in the group is prepped for the discussion.

- As students read, have them mark interesting passages and jot down open-ended discussion questions. They will need to pose several good discussion topics during the lesson, so this prep is essential. The text is your choice, so pick something that will work to further your current unit of study.

The Lesson

Slide 1

TITLE: **Saving the Last Word**

Slide 2

➔ Begin with a celebration of the excellent preparation and thinking that you've observed.

Slide 3

➔ Project and read aloud.

➔ *Do you notice this also?*

Slide 4

➔ Continue to describe what you've observed:

  ▪ *Typically, when one person says it all (usually the person who brought up the topic), the rest of the group nods in agreement and moves on to a new discussion topic. Besides the fact that no in-depth discussion is taking place, quieter group members who might have some interesting and valuable ideas to share can't get a word in.*

➔ Conclude:

  ▪ *Today, we are going to try out a strategy that will help you hear everyone's voice and refine your discussions.*

Slide 5

➔ Monitor this count-off closely. Though it seems obvious, make sure students count off in a circle.

➔ Without making that direction *very* clear, we guarantee that at least one group will count off in a zigzag fashion, which will make it nearly impossible for members to easily follow the upcoming directions.

Slide 6

➔ Have all the number ones raise their hands. They will be the discussion starters, the members who throw out a question or passage for discussion.

➔ Explain that they will need to ask everyone to turn to the same text page and paragraph that they are looking at.

➔ Once the rest of the group is there, the starter should read the passage aloud or ask an open-ended discussion question. Say:

  ▪ *Okay, discussion starters, throw your item out to the group, but wait a moment to begin the discussion because we're going to try to change things up a bit today.*

Slide 7

➔ Now say:

  ▪ *Discussion starters, I bet you could say a lot about the question or passage you just offered to your group, but right now you can only say one thing: "Save the last word for me."*

➔ Have fun with this; encourage the discussion starters to be dramatic.

➔ *Turn to your group, say the phrase, and then have everyone else silently think about their responses.*

Slide 8

➔ *Now, discussion starters, you must listen carefully as the other members in your group answer the question you posed or comment on the passage you picked.*

➔ *Group members, try not just to repeat what the previous person said. Add to a previous idea or come up with an entirely new thought that makes sense.*

Slide 9

➔ Emphasize that once everyone else in the group has shared, it's the responsibility of the discussion starter to keep the discussion going.

➔ The starter can:

  ▪ Ask an open-ended follow-up question based on what others said

  ▪ Build (piggyback) on the ideas shared

  ▪ Bring up a related idea or text passage that will get members talking

  ▪ Just make the comment she has been dying to share right from the beginning

Slide 10

➔ Now say:

  ▪ *We're going to try this again. For this round, keep the same discussion starter. Starters, all of you are going to bring up a new topic for discussion, so remember that you need to start by telling everyone where to look in the text before you ask your question or read a passage. Then, just like last time, all you can say at first is, "Save the last word for me." Don't forget to make it dramatic! Before we start, review the steps.*

➜ Give students a minute to study the steps.

➜ *Are there any questions? Okay, discussion starters, you're on!*

➜ As groups discuss, monitor and eavesdrop.

➜ If possible, drag around a chair or stool so that you can plop into any group and observe members at eye level.

➜ Most likely, you will notice that the last person to share will not have much to talk about; everything that could have been said has already been said. This is completely predictable, and the next slides offer a solution to this problem.

Slide 11

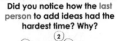

➜ Project and read aloud.

➜ Give groups a minute to confer and ask them to share their explanations for the cause of this problem.

Slide 12

➜ Most likely, students will mention that it's hard to think of a lot of good ideas fast and that it's really hard for the last person to think of something that hasn't already been said.

➜ Say:

■ *In a moment, we are going to continue discussion—but we're also going to change a couple of things. First, the order in which you answer is going to rotate. That means if you were a number one just now, you'll be a number two this time. Review your earlier count-off and then figure out your new numbers for the rotation.*

➜ Give groups a minute.

■ *Any questions?*

■ *Second, in this next round of discussion, you're going to be observing a wait time before anyone can answer. The new discussion starter (that's the person who is now number one) has to count up to five before number two can give the first answer. During this wait time you want to work hard to think of all the ideas you could share as well as lines in the text you might point out to support your opinion.*

Slide 13

➜ *Read through the steps again. Wait a minute for silent reading. Don't forget that you've rotated numbers. Go ahead and continue discussion. And when you are finished with this round, rotate again: new discussion starter, new answering order. And whenever it's your turn to be the discussion starter, it's your job to try to keep the discussion going after that initial round of sharing. Any questions? Work to keep your discussion going until I call time.*

→ Return to your monitoring.

→ Don't be afraid to intervene if you see the same talkative person answering first or if you see members forget to say, "Save the last word for me."

→ Intervene as well if you see members forget to add the count of five wait time.

→ If you observe most groups following all of the instructions, including speaking role rotation and wait time, there is no need to interrupt the class again. As you monitor, just inform groups that they "look good" and to keep going with their discussion as they follow the Save the Last Word instructions.

Slide 14

→ Give groups a couple of minutes to review their discussion.

→ Next, randomly call on some members to share.

Slide 15

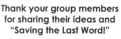

→ Give groups a minute to list some skills they used.

→ Then have them decide which one made the biggest difference in improving discussion and report to the rest of the class.

→ Often, groups do not say exactly the same thing, which makes this share interesting.

Slide 16

→ End with a thank you and a celebratory high five!

Further Comments

Save the Last Word focuses on making sure everyone shares equally in listening and contributing.

Save the Last Word is a strategy that focuses on making sure everyone shares equally in listening and contributing. As we said in Chapter 2, any new skill feels unnatural and makes the conversation seem forced and stiff. Don't buy the complaint from the kids that Save the Last Word is ruining their conversations. What they really mean is that the "talkers" are no longer allowed to dominate. Reassure the groups that they can stop using Save the Last Word when you notice that everyone in the group is carefully listening and equally contributing interesting, meaty thoughts.

LESSON 18: WRITE-AROUNDS

Why Use It?

When kids engage in write-arounds, every student is either writing or reading about the assigned topic, the whole time.

Written conversations potentially engage every single kid in the room. There's no waiting required—or allowed! When kids engage in write-arounds, every student is either writing or reading about the assigned topic, the whole time. Compare this to whole-class discussions, where too often a couple of teacher-pleasing volunteers wave their hands, while everyone else sleeps and remembers nothing. We often moan about kids' lack of motivation, their inattentiveness, their propensity toward snoozing—but if we deploy apathy-bashing classroom structures, everyone wins. This one is a keeper.

When to Use It

Any kind of discussion that students might have out loud in small groups, they can also have in writing. So the usefulness of the write-around is *daily*. While this strategy does have one of the longest slide shows in this resource, and requires careful training, that doesn't mean it is an end-of-the-year thing. Smokey and his wife, Elaine, have written a whole book about the many uses and variations of written conversations (2013). As they assert, this is not a fad or a treat or a one-time diversion. In many classrooms where we work, teachers use different forms of letter writing through the week, over every month, and all year long.

Preparation

- While written conversations can be done digitally, using tablets, laptops, or web spaces like Edmodo, we prefer to train kids with paper and pencil first. So be sure you have old-school writing materials at hand when you commence your first "write-arounds."

The Lesson

Slide 1

TITLE: **Write-Arounds**

➜ Just let students enjoy the photo briefly.

➜ If it seems appropriate, you can ask volunteers to briefly share a time when they got in trouble for writing a note in class.

Slide 2

➜ Read the slide; it simply explains the activity to your kids.

➜ Form groups of three to five, as numbers in your classroom dictate. Groups of three are ideal for write-arounds.

➜ Note that when the writing happens, there might only be three passes of paper, no matter the size of the group. This just means that not everyone in the groups of four or five will write to everyone else—but it still works fine. When the kids switch to out-loud conversation, everyone's voice gets heard by everyone.

Slide 3

➜ The salutation can use names, which we believe encourages friendliness and support in the classroom. Or you can invite playfulness by letting kids cook up their own salutations: "Hi, Guys," "Dear Gang," "Hello, Classmates," "Greetings, People of Earth," etc.

➜ The full-size sheet is needed because kids will hopefully fill both sides, or close to it.

➜ If you use note cards or smaller scraps of paper, it becomes difficult for groups to keep track of multiple sheets as they pass letters around.

Slide 4

➜ Kids need to sign their names every time they compose or answer a letter. Real names or identifiable aliases are preferred. Our favorite write-around signoff ever, from a boy in Arkansas:

This IS,

Justin Adams

Slide 5

➜ Write legibly.

➜ Keep the pressure light on this; the issue is readability, not handwriting or cursive. For some kids, the simple act of writing is hard. It is not the end of the world if a kid has to whisper to a partner, "What does this mean?" while pointing to a puzzling word.

→ Tell kids that written conversations are not for a grade (except for participation or good faith effort) and that spelling and grammar will not be scored. This is one-draft, unedited, writing to learn, with no time given for revision or proofreading.

→ However, to prevent kids from wandering off the assigned topic, we suggest you *do* say, "I will be collecting these."

→ Really stress that drawing one's thoughts is a totally legitimate way to join in a write-around. We often say:

- *Use a cartoon, diagram, stick-figure scene, timeline, or map—anything that helps you get your thinking on the page. Remember, with a drawing you can also use labels, captions, talk balloons, or thought balloons to help get your ideas across.*

→ We've found that this graphic alternative really invites in English language learners, some kids with IEPs, students of a more visual bent, and young people who simply are slower text producers.

Slide 6

→ At first, kids may not understand the idea of writing continuously until time is called. So we'll explain:

- *You're only going to write for about a minute and a half, but I want you to keep writing that whole time. It's not fair to write "this is dumb," and put your pen down. Your pen should be moving the whole minute and a half. How can you do that? Write down more comments or connections to the topic or to what your partners said. Write down questions. You can even start a friendly argument, if you like—just keep the written conversation going.*

→ This is supposed to be a silent activity. If some kids start chatting, we just tell them, *Keep it in writing!*

→ It's almost inevitable that people will talk some when exchanging letters (it is a normal, sociable thing to do), but encourage them again to *save it for your next letter.*

Slide 7

→ Feel free to substitute your own kid-friendly, highly debatable topic or text excerpt here.

→ The think time is important, so allow thirty to sixty seconds.

Slide 8

→ This extends the individual, silent thinking time.

Slide 9

→ Notice how carefully we are creeping up on the command: *Start writing*.

→ Once they begin, written conversations have a tremendous amount of positive social pressure. Within ninety seconds, every kid has to deliver a note to a buddy, and be ready to immediately answer a letter from another classmate. So we want to be really sure that every kid is ready to write when we do give the signal.

Slide 10

→ Here's another support for slow-starting writers. We call these "safety net starters," because they are designed to support kids who "just can't think of anything to write about," even when the topic is relevant and (we think) engaging. We are careful with the instructions:

- *This is not a list of five things you must write about. These are different ways you could begin your first letter if you don't have anything else in mind yet. If you've already got an idea, go right ahead with it.*

Slide 11

→ If kids are highly engaged, go ahead and let them write a minute or two longer. They will have more text to discuss in the next letter.

→ Wait until the slower producing writers have at least got a few lines on the page before you call a pass.

→ With fifteen seconds left, we read this warning gently and quietly, so kids can in fact finish the thought or sentence on which they are working.

Slide 12

→ For the best results (and least confusion), tell kids: "pass to the right" (or left). When students are sitting in groups that are basically round or square, this is the simplest.

Slide 13

→ These instructions remind kids that this is much like receiving a real letter, e-mail, or text. You read it, and then you answer it.

Slide 14

→ These instructions are especially useful the first time kids engage in a write-around; you won't need to dwell on them in the future.

Slide 15

→ We leave the writing possibilities projected to support those kids who still need a reminder.

Slide 16

→ Another time warning. Sometimes at this stage we playfully invite kids to shake their poor, tired wrists before exchanging papers.

Slide 17

→ Kids will need a little more time in this round, since they have two letters to read (and if you go on to additional notes, even more). So do extend the time to allow for more reading.

→ If you'll be stopping the letter exchange after this next round of notes, you may choose to add:

   ▪ *This will be our last letter for today, so if you can find a way to finish or tie together the conversation, please do.*

Slide 18

→ Yes, we offer response options again for partners who still need support.

Slide 19

→ Give the final "time is running out" warning.

Slide 20

→ Keep it quiet and allow time for kids to fully digest what the other two kids have written (or three, or however many joined in).

→ We sometimes say:

   ▪ *This paper holds a conversation that you started about ten minutes ago. So now take a look and see what other people said, based on your ideas.*

Slide 21

→ Some groups can switch from written to oral conversation without a hitch.

→ Others hesitate, wondering how to start talking. This step ensures that all groups will have something specific to discuss when the discussion "goes live."

Slide 22

→ Here we give kids a choice of how to begin their out-loud conversation.

→ Give them about three minutes of discussion time as you circulate and listen in to groups.

→ If you hear a student make an interesting comment in a group, you can later invite that kid to chip it into the whole-class discussion coming up next.

Slide 23

→ These prompts are intentionally general.

→ If kids have been writing about a narrower or more curriculum-based topic, you can pose more targeted questions.

Slide 24

→ You won't use this step every time your kids have a written discussion, but it is important to do once or twice as kids are learning the strategy.

→ If you make the two-column chart as we suggest on the slide, some very important characteristics of written conversations—as compared to out-loud, small-group discussions—should come up, such as:

- *No one can dominate the conversation*
- *Everyone gets the same amount of time*
- *No one can interrupt you*
- *Writing can be more thoughtful, less impulsive*
- *There's no side talk to distract you*

→ And see what else your kids think of.

Slide 25

→ Writing buddies forever!

LESSON 19: GALLERY WALK

Why Use It?

Gallery Walk is one of our favorite "up and thinking" activities that has kids moving actively around the room, talking and thinking.

As the lesson explains, galleries are places people go to admire and interact with the work of artists and creators. Applied to the classroom, Gallery Walk is one of our favorite "up and thinking" activities that has kids moving actively around the room, talking and thinking about other students' work on a curricular topic. No, they don't go crazy when we let them out of their seats, as long as we have provided the ethic of appreciation and provided careful procedures—just like they do in real art galleries.

When to Use It

This is the go-to structure when kids have created large or graphic work that needs to be shared with many fellow students—or the whole class.

Preparation

- Duplicate copies of an interesting short article, story, or poem. All students will need their own copy.
- Have all the materials ready to go: large poster paper (you may have to go to a primary classroom to get this stuff), colored markers, tape, and pads of sticky notes.
- Think about where in the room (or in the hall) you could create a well-spaced array of posters so small groups can move freely among them.

The Lesson

Slide 1

TITLE: **Gallery Walk**

Slide 2

→ This introduces the culture and purpose of art galleries. You can ask who has been to a museum or art gallery and have volunteers describe the purpose of these institutions.

Slide 3

→ Have kids regard the walls for just a second. They may be blank; they may be festooned with materials.

→ Talk about what it would take to get *this* wall ready to be a gallery.

→ You should already have your own idea about where kids' drawings could be placed; maybe some decorations will need to be temporarily taken down, moved, or covered up. Think about traffic patterns and potential obstacles around the display areas.

Slide 4

→ Trios work best for this activity—having more than three kids trying to write on the same piece of paper, no matter how large, rarely works well.

Slide 5

→ Teach this simple text-coding tool (or another quick annotation strategy of your preference) *before* handing out the article, so kids don't start reading before you have given the instructions.

→ If your students are not familiar with the active-reader mindset of "stop, think, and react," take your time and show them how to leave tracks of their thinking as they read.

Slide 6

→ Give kids about three minutes (one minute each) to chat about their initial responses to the text.

→ Encourage them to refer to their codes to restart the discussion if conversation lags.

Slide 7

→ Now it's time for kids to "go graphic," turning some aspect of their thoughts about the text into a drawing, cartoon, diagram, stick-figure scene, model, timeline, or other visual representation.

→ At this stage, each student is working alone on her own section of the chart paper. Allow three minutes as you circulate and support, and keep kids' hands from crashing into each other on the page.

Slide 8

→ Now have each group hang its charts at an easy-to-read height, leaving enough space between each one for groups to gather and rotate between them.

→ Naturally, be ready with tape, pins, or other appropriate hangers.

Slide 9

→ Decide how you'll steer groups to the "other kids'" posters they will study and respond to first.

→ This can simply be "the one to the right of yours," or you can set up some more exotic rotation.

→ Be sure all students bring sticky notes and a pen so they can leave their comments on the wall beside their classmates' posters. Alternatively, you can have student "visitors" write comments directly in whatever margins exist on the paper itself.

Slide 10

→ Explain that kids are first supposed to read most or all of what was written on the paper:

- *Try to notice your own responses, connections, questions, agreements, and doubts as you look.*

- *Next, share and discuss these thoughts with your team.*

- *Last, each person jot down and leave your own most valuable thought for the other team. Don't forget to sign your name.*

→ Time this activity by watching the students' progress. Three minutes is usually plenty for the first stop; more time will be needed at subsequent stations.

Slide 11

→ Now it gets interesting. When you rotate kids to the next team's chart, they will be able to study not just the original authors' illustrations, but also the written comments from the team that just visited.

→ This means you have to allow more time for kids to digest the additional material, chat, and then write their individual comments.

→ If you love complexity, you can then go one or two more rounds, with more material to be studied at every stop. In the baseline lesson, kids visit two other groups and then return to their own poster.

Slide 12

→ Now kids are back at their own posters with at least six sticky notes to read and discuss—and get ready to respond to when the whole class debriefs the exercise.

Slide 13

→ Monitor and assist as kids choose one sticky note each.

Slide 14

→ Invite volunteers from different groups to share a comment and explain how it deepened their thinking about their drawing or the article.

Slide 15

→ Quickly debrief the process, and share ways of using it even more effectively in the future.

Chapter 8

Ongoing Discussion Groups

Many of our most powerful teaching structures require small groups of kids to work together, not just for a few minutes or one class period, but over several days or even weeks. This kind of extended collaboration is required by structures such as:

- Literature circles
- Book clubs
- Group inquiry projects
- Research teams
- Project-based learning

This lesson family lays the groundwork for such activities by explicitly pre-troubleshooting all the problems that can plague newly formed groups:

- Staying on task
- Involving everyone
- Maintaining a supportive climate
- Purposefully reflecting and improving

There are five lessons in this group, each with a fairly self-explanatory title:

Lesson 20. Establishing Group Ground Rules

Lesson 21. Overcoming Off-Task Triggers

Lesson 22. Goal Setting for Group Improvement

Lesson 23. Reinforcing Collaboration With Table Cards

Lesson 24. Compliment Cards

LESSON 20: ESTABLISHING GROUP GROUND RULES

Why Use It?

One of the reasons why kids complain about working in groups is the specter of group grades and the uneven division of labor. There's the member who comes fully prepared and the hitchhiker who's hoping to ride everyone else's coattails without doing any of the work. While it's important to acknowledge this reality, it's also important to point out that work teams are a fact of life, so figuring out how to solve this problem is more practical than hoping you can spend your entire life working alone. And even if some kid points out that she plans on being a research scientist in a solitary lab (tell *that* to Pfizer), most of your students are still planning to get married and possibly raise a family, so everyone will eventually have the opportunity to negotiate some Ground Rules.

When to Use It

If group members are going to be working together for a while, it is imperative that everyone be accountable to the group.

If group members are going to be working together for a while *and* their project will be dependent upon completing work outside of class (this is typical for literature circles and many group projects), it is imperative that everyone be accountable to the group. The best way to establish that accountability is with the creation of Ground Rules. When we form long-term work groups, we always start with a friendly Membership Grid discussion (page 213 in the Resources and www.corwin.com/teachingsocialskills) and then move straight to having each group develop its own set of rules. That way, everyone in the group knows the expectations of all members from the very start.

Preparation

- Decide ahead of time how students will form longer-term work groups of three to five.
- Decide how members will record their group's Ground Rules: on paper you hand out, on their brand-new tablets, on loose-leaf retrieved from their binders, etc.

The Lesson

Slide 1

TITLE: **Establishing Group Ground Rules**

Slide 2

→ Ask: *Ever work in a group that could have been better?*

Slide 3

→ Have students think for a minute: *What are the behaviors that make group work difficult?*

→ Share the problems they've run across—without mentioning any names, of course!

→ Typically, students will mention some deficiencies of past group members:

- Is not prepared
- Does not talk
- Lets other people do the work
- Ignores group
- Wanders around the room
- Brings distracting/irrelevant/inappropriate items to meetings
- Sleeps
- Monopolizes the conversation
- Refuses to listen to other members' ideas
- Criticizes ideas with put-downs

→ You don't need to write these down (no need to get fixated on all of life's past disappointments). Just listen to what volunteers have to say.

Slide 4

→ Say:

- *Let's figure out how a group might avoid some of these problems.*

Slide 5

When you are working with your group, what are some Ground Rules you'd like everyone to stick to?

→ Let kids think a minute and elaborate:

- Silently think for a minute about how you would want other members in your group to act.

- What behaviors would make a group great instead of a bust?

- What does each member need to do so that the work gets shared equally and your meetings are fun and productive?

Slide 6

With your group, negotiate the five most important rules for getting along and getting the job done.

→ Have students meet with their groups to negotiate their list of Ground Rules.

→ If members of a group ask if they can have fewer than five, that's fine. If they want more than five, tell them to pick out their top five and then see how the meetings go.

→ Later on, they can always swap one rule out for another or add to the list; but to start out, it's easier to work with fewer rules.

Slide 7

Let's hear each group's rules.

→ When groups report out, remind the rest of the groups to listen carefully.

→ Students will find it interesting how similar the rules are from group to group, yet almost every group will have at least one rule that reflects its individuality.

→ After the large-group share, have members return to their huddle for a minute and confirm or revise their rules. After hearing the other groups' rules, they now might realize they want to swap one rule for another.

→ To what kinds of rules do groups typically agree?

- Come prepared and ready to work

- Listen to each other's ideas

- Stay on task

- Ask good, open-ended questions

- Do all the reading and notes by the due date

- Address each other by name

- Include everyone in the discussion

- Make this group Home Court

- Be friendly

- Treat others respectfully

Slide 8

From now on, remember to review your Ground Rules at the start of each group meeting.

→ Say something like this:

- *To keep your group moving forward, members should review these rules before each discussion so all members contribute positively!*

Slide 9

→ Say:

- *Don't forget—you negotiated these rules so that everyone in your group will do their best work and not drive any of the other members nuts.*

- *Your group's goal is to avoid those negative experiences you described a little bit earlier.*

- *If your group runs into some problems, do not come to me first for solutions. Look for answers within the group, probably by renegotiating your Ground Rules so that they work better. Your Ground Rules are living documents that can be revised when necessary.*

Slide 10

→ If groups are doing academic work together the same day they establish their Ground Rules, have them return to their rules at the end of the meeting and offer compliments to each other based on a rule that each member modeled in an exceptional way. Mostly likely, members will have difficulty choosing because Ground Rules often guide members to their most courteous behavior!

→ Conclude with members thanking each other for their careful listening and thoughtfulness as they developed their Ground Rules. End with a "thumbs up."

Variation

→ If you are concerned that Ground Rules will not be enough to keep groups on the rails, you might also have them determine a "liability policy" for kids who become a negative asset. Now, instead of you kicking a nonproductive student out of a group, let the kids determine the consequences. When confronted with the issue of the slacking member, it's surprising how tough groups can be.

→ While most decide not to excommunicate a member on the first offense, most groups decide to limit the interaction. For example:

- *If you're not prepared or you are distracting us from the work, we'll let you stay this time but only if you are silent.*

- *On the second offense, the member is removed from the group to catch up and prepare for the next meeting.*

- *The third offense usually results in an intervention with the group, offending member, and the teacher.*

→ Sometimes groups want problem members to be singled out in public ways: wearing a dunce cap or a button that says, "I'm a loser." Of course, we always nix those ideas; but we can't help but wonder what past class gave them that idea.

LESSON 21: OVERCOMING OFF-TASK TRIGGERS

Why Use It?

Even with a good set of initial Ground Rules in place, sooner or later, any group can go off on a tangent. (This applies to kids and most definitely to teachers in faculty meetings.) Sometimes the digression starts with a student's personal connection to the content material, but before you know it, the focus derails and everyone is telling stories about their middle school field trips. To a certain extent, these detours actually promote group solidarity; kids are engaging in impromptu Membership Grid–type sharing. However, when off-task conversations dominate a group's time, members just aren't getting the academic task at hand done.

A related off-course scenario is when groups fragment into subgroups. In a trio, two kids are talking and one kid is left out. In a group of four, the members split into pairs, each having its own conversation and ignoring the other pair. Instead of giving up and sighing, "I knew groups would never work," describe your observations to the kids and turn this problem back to them to solve.

When to Use It

This lesson can be used with a whole class if all the groups seem to be falling off task, or it can be used with just one group as a coaching intervention.

This lesson can be used with a whole class if all the groups seem to be falling off task, or it can be used with just one group as a coaching intervention. While we usually do model this problem-solving procedure with the whole class, you could just as easily sit down with the one group that is having problems and lead it through this lesson (bring your laptop and use the slides!) while the rest of the groups continue on productively.

Preparation

- Decide ahead of time how students will form ongoing work groups of three to five.
- Each member will need a blank sheet of paper for creating the Off-Task Behavior chart shown in Slide 2.

The Lesson

Slide 1

TITLE: **Overcoming Off-Task Triggers**

→ Start by describing a few of the off-task behaviors you've observed as groups work together.

→ Say something like this:

- *A little bit of off-task behavior sometimes actually helps the group to have fun and bond together. On the other hand, a lot of time devoted to off-task activity undermines the group. It frustrates members and prevents the group from completing the work well.*

Slide 2

→ Pass out the blank paper and show students how to fold it into three columns.

→ Label the first column Off-Task Behaviors.

→ Say something like this:

- *I've mentioned some of the off-task behaviors I've seen. What off-task behavior is your group struggling with?*

- *Take a couple of minutes to talk with your group and recall your recent meetings.*

- *Jot down the behaviors that kept you from staying on the topic and getting the work done.*

- *I think you can come up with a list all on your own, but if you are having trouble I can definitely help you get that list started!*

Slide 3

→ Explain that off-task behaviors just don't happen; something triggers the behavior.

→ Have students review the behaviors they listed in Column 1 and discuss what triggers them, listing those triggers in Column 2. Give them approximately three to five minutes.

→ Here are some additional examples of what students may list.

Off-Task Behaviors	Off-Task Triggers	Solutions
<ul><li>Talking to people in groups nearby.</li><li>Talking about stuff that has nothing to do with the book.</li><li>Spinning paper around on pencil.</li><li>Groups breaking down into subgroups, with members ignoring each other.</li></ul>	<ul><li>Making eye contact with friends instead of staying focused on the group.</li><li>Thinking of a personal connection to the text.</li><li>Feeling bored, left out of the discussion.</li><li>Some members are not prepared.</li><li>Don't know all members well, so we talk to our friends.</li><li>Some members don't talk, so we end up leaving them out, ignoring them—giving up.</li></ul>	

➔ Of course, the behaviors listed in the first column could have many other triggers than the examples listed. That's why it's so important for kids to figure out exactly what the triggers are for them.

Slide 4

➔ Ask students to discuss how to recognize and avoid the triggers they've uncovered. Their solutions go in the last column.

➔ As groups work, monitor their progress. If a group is struggling, say:

  ▪ *It looks like you're stuck. Would you like me to give you a couple of suggestions?*

➔ Ninety percent of the time the above statement will get the unfocused group back on track because members would much rather solve the problem on their own than have you tell them what to do!

➔ Once groups have their charts completed, take a moment for each group to report on its triggers and solutions. Remind the kids there is no need to mention any names. After each group reports out, say:

  ▪ *Now that you've all reported out, take a final look at your chart.*

  ▪ *Is there anything you heard from another group that you can add to your own plan to make it more solid?*

  ▪ *Take a moment to review it and add solutions.*

Slide 5

➔ Ideally, you've done this lesson right before students are going to have a meeting so that they can immediately try out their off-task trigger plans.

➔ After their group discussion, have them review their chart again and see how they did.

→ Subsequently, groups should always review this chart—and their preexisting Ground Rules—at the beginning of each meeting.

Slide 6

→ Any improvement in our interaction is always reason to celebrate!

LESSON 22: GOAL SETTING FOR GROUP IMPROVEMENT

Why Use It?

Groups that continue to improve also learn more and become more academically agile—and that includes improving test performance.

Even when a group is humming, it can always refine the tune. Members need to always be cognizant of *why* their group is functioning well, remembering that a good group doesn't happen by accident. A group is productive not just because of "chemistry," but because of the skills and behaviors members are using. And every group can keep getting better, so members need to discuss what they can do to "kick it up a notch" (which makes us wonder what Emeril is doing these days). But here's the bottom line: improving a group's collaborative efforts doesn't just translate into a pleasant, enjoyable meeting. Groups that continue to improve also learn more and become more academically agile—and that includes improving test performance.

When to Use It

As many of our lessons model, it is beneficial for members to reflect back at the end of any group meeting to reflect on how they operated. At the first meetings of newly formed groups, we like to focus solely on positive performance aspects that reflect skillful social interaction. In subsequent meetings, groups continue to document skillful contributions but also begin to analyze their collaboration and think about what behavior or collaborative skill might improve the next meeting.

Preparation

- This lesson assumes that students have already been working in longer-standing teams of three to five.
- Plan to introduce this lesson immediately after some group work has taken place.
- Decide how students will record their group's goal-setting notes.

The Lesson

TITLE: **Goal Setting for Group Improvement**

→ Begin by saying that groups can always improve their performance, but you noticed a lot of positive behaviors as you monitored members while they worked together today.

→ Say something like this:

- *I'm going to give your groups a couple of minutes to write down three group accomplishments. To get ready, think about this:*
  - *What behaviors really helped your group today get the job done?*
  - *What kept everyone involved and enjoying each other's company?*
- *When you think about the skills your group used, try to be as specific as possible. Instead of saying "we cooperated," say:*
  - *"We kept focused on each other."*
  - *"We used good eye contact."*
  - *"We asked lots of open-ended follow-ups."*
  - *"We remembered to thank each other."*
- *I watched your work today. No one threw a punch or stormed out of the room, so I know every group can come up with at least three behaviors for their list, and if you think of more, be sure to write them down!*

→ Give the groups two to three minutes to write down their three accomplishments.

→ As you monitor, ask them to read what they noted. When groups give answers like "We participated," or "We cooperated," or "We listened," prod them to go further by asking them what that really means:

- *There are a hundred different skills that groups use when they are cooperating. What are three things you did that showed you really cooperated?*
- *Start talking about those specific skills you used, and in a couple of minutes I'll check by to see what you've got.*

➜ If students still seem to have difficulty putting specific labels on their interaction skills, send them back to their notes on Home Court, Friendliness and Support, and Good Partner Traits. What does cooperation look like? What does it sound like?

Slide 4

➜ Once groups have their lists, ask each group to share one specific success with the class.

➜ Encourage succeeding groups to mention a different kind of success, if possible.

➜ It's important for everyone to hear this because:

- It reinforces all the different skills that go into making successful collaborative work.

- Hearing what the other groups say helps groups recognize skills they use but didn't jot down.

- Groups will hear skills that maybe they need to work on.

Slide 5

➜ *The flip side of skills successes are skills needing improvement.*

Slide 6

➜ Project and read aloud.

➜ Then say:

- *Everyone think about this silently for a minute.*

- *What is the one thing that would really improve your group's next meeting?*

➜ As groups become more experienced, they will become better at pinpointing weaknesses, but in the beginning the kids might have a little trouble. If that is the case, introduce this slide by describing what you observed without pointing to specific groups:

- *If you are having trouble deciding what to work on, here are some weaknesses I noticed:*

  - *Groups discussed without going back to the text.*

  - *Some groups split off into subgroups.*

  - *One member kept bringing up discussion items rather than taking turns.*

  - *Group members forgot to use "Save the Last Word for Me."*

  - *Some members talked a lot more than others.*

➜ *Turn back to your group, share your ideas, and agree on the one goal you think would make the biggest difference.*

Slide 7

→ Explain that just picking out a weakness is not enough to change how a group functions.

→ Tell members that they also need to figure out exactly how they will *act differently* in order to improve that weak skill.

→ Remind students to be very specific in describing behaviors needed to meet their goal.

→ Remind them of the charts we did about Friendliness and Support. The posters may be hanging right on your wall (see pages 58–61).

→ Tell groups they should always brainstorm the *actual phrases* they will say when trying to meet their new goal. For example, if a group keeps forgetting to use "Save the Last Word for Me," it might brainstorm these phrases:

- "You asked the question, now you need to listen to our answers."
- "Don't forget, you give your opinion last."
- "Let's all count to five before anyone answers."
- "I answered first last time; who gets to go first this time?"
- "Let the person who answered last go first this time."

Slide 8

→ Once groups have their plans ready, have each group quickly share an improvement goal with the rest of the class.

→ Encourage succeeding groups to mention a different kind of goal, if possible.

→ Knowing that all groups can find ways to improve helps students move to a more thoughtful, reflective way of looking at their interactions.

Slide 9

→ Nothing smooths over the rough edges and makes the final moments of a meeting glow like a sincere thanks. When you're working at school, how many times do you get thanked during the day? Probably not enough— and it's the same for the kids. Even if it's a little staged, being thanked still feels good!

At the beginning of students' next group meeting:

Slides 6 and 7

→ Show Slides 6 and 7 again. Have members review their improvement goal—and accompanying behaviors—from the last meeting. It's not a bad idea for each group to repeat its goals to the rest of the class, in a kind of public commitment.

After that group meeting:

Slide 10

→ Show Slide 10.

→ Have groups review their goals again and talk about how it went.

- *Did you use the behaviors you planned?*

→ As groups discuss, monitor and check in.

→ If students say they met the goal but you observed otherwise, say:

- *How do you know for sure you met your goal?*

- *What's the evidence?*

- *Work on recalling the things each person said and did that reflected the skill.*

- *If your group has met the goal, then everyone is using the skill successfully.*

- *I'll check back with you in a couple of minutes to see what you came up with.*

→ When you check back, the group will probably have figured out that members need to keep working on the same goal. If not, then go ahead and share what you observed.

→ End by saying:

- *I think you should probably keep working on this goal.*

- *However, if your group truly thinks you've accomplished it, then what is your new improvement goal?*

- *Figure that out and then brainstorm a list of accompanying behaviors that will help you meet it.*

→ For the groups that *did* successfully meet their goal:

- Instruct them to examine their functioning and set a new goal.

- If a group struggles to come up with a new goal, suggest a useful skill that takes quite a while to master, for example:

  - Remember to actually say Friendliness and Support phrases.

  - Consistently ask follow-up questions when people share ideas.

Slide 11

→ Group skill improvement is hard work that should be celebrated!

Further Comments

The Group Meeting Procedures checklist (on page 214 in the Resources and www.corwin.com/teachingsocialskills) will help groups remember their beginning and end-of-discussion responsibilities.

LESSON 23: REINFORCING COLLABORATION WITH TABLE CARDS

Why Use It?

Collaborative skill table cards nudge students into using necessary skills more consistently by making each of them an expert.

Even though students can learn how to analyze their group's interaction patterns and set goals for improvement, it takes a lot of practice to incorporate a new discussion skill into one's behavior. Also, trying to use a new skill can feel a bit uncomfortable, so it's human nature just to ease back into our old ways. However, old ways don't refine group collaboration; using and improving interaction skills does. Collaborative skill table cards are a way to nudge students into using the necessary skills more consistently by making each of them an expert.

When to Use It

This is a lesson best used after ongoing groups have met a couple of times. Members are starting to know each other and also to recognize their group's strengths and weaknesses. This recognition enables members to then choose the skills most needed to strengthen their group.

Preparation

- Do this with students who are already working in groups of three to five.
- Decide how students will record their group's skill notes: on paper you hand out, loose-leaf retrieved from their binders, or tablets.
- Supply large, 8 × 5–inch index cards (8-1/2 × 11 card stock is even better) and pencils with erasers. Each student will need a card.
- Provide students an assortment of markers, crayons, or colored pencils so they can make eye-catching table cards.

The Lesson

Slide 1

TITLE: **Reinforcing Collaboration With Table Cards**

Slide 2

➔ Compliment students on how well they've been working together so far.

➔ Explain that there is always an opportunity for improving and refining their discussion skills.

Slide 3

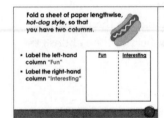

➔ Project and read aloud. Have students set up their papers.

Slide 4

➔ Explain that there are two sets of skills that improve discussion:
  ▪ Skills that make discussion fun
  ▪ Skills that make discussion interesting

➔ A really skilled group makes use of both. Go ahead and give a couple of examples:

Fun	Interesting
• Support and Friendliness • Using members' names • Complimenting ideas	• Picking good passages/topics • Asking open-ended questions • Making personal connections that relate

➔ Once groups understand, challenge them to brainstorm lots of specific skills that could be listed under these two categories.

→ We like to set a minimum number. For example: five new skill ideas that don't repeat the initial examples.

→ As students brainstorm, monitor and be on the lookout for vague descriptors: cooperation, working together, listening.

→ Intervene and instruct groups to break those big behaviors down to the observable subskills that are required to "cooperate." For example:

   ▪ *What does cooperation look like? What does it sound like?*

Slide 5

→ Create a class list, just as we've done in previous lessons (Home Court, Good Partner Traits).

→ Assign a Student Scribe so you are free to manage the class as needed.

→ Display the class list as it develops, using the projector or board.

→ Instruct everyone to add new items to the lists they originally made in their groups.

Slide 6

→ Reconvene groups to determine which skills would most benefit their own group.

→ Ask groups to pick out as many skills as they have group members. In other words, if a group has four members, then it needs to pick out four skills, three group members, three skills, etc.

→ Encourage groups to choose a balance between the Fun skills and the Interesting skills. Without this instruction, kids will predictably lean heavily on the Fun skills, sometimes ignoring the Interesting skills completely.

→ Question groups if you notice them making unbalanced selections. It might be that a group chose all Fun skills because members haven't been getting along very well. If you've noticed that as well, don't argue with them. Their decision to focus on using names, keeping everyone involved, and being friendly and supportive could be the right call.

Slide 7

→ Instruct groups to negotiate who will take charge of which skill.

→ We encourage members to choose skills with which they are a little weak, since the only way to get good at a skill is to practice it a lot. Becoming that skill's expert will help them grow individually into stronger group members.

Slide 8

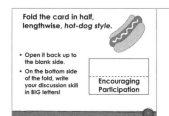

→ Pass out the index cards.

→ Talk students through the directions of folding and writing their skill on the front of the card in big letters that everyone can read easily.

➔ Have everyone sketch their cards out in pencil first, so mistakes can be corrected.

➔ Create your own card ahead of time; using an example is always very helpful.

➔ Walk around the room and show the kids your example, or project it

Slide 9

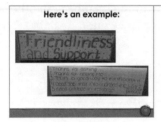

➔ Make sure students understand that they need to be able to read the *back* of the card, while their members need to be able to read the *front*.

➔ Emphasize the importance of big lettering and clear legibility.

➔ Explicitly point out on the slide how the lettering for the front of the cards appears upside down to the notes when the card is opened flat.

➔ As students work at writing phrases they will say on the back side of the cards, remind them that they are creating items that would fall under the Sounds Like side of the Discussion Skill T-Charts they have made before.

➔ Skill experts do not need to complete their cards alone. Encourage groups to brainstorm phrases for each other to use on their cards. Talking about the different skills together is a good thing!

Slide 10

➔ As students think about the skill, show them this example as well. Encourage artists to make the public side of their card an eye-catching reminder while the back side serves as their script.

Slide 11

➔ Once members have executed the correct card format—and proofread their lettering—make the markers, crayons, and colored pencils available.

➔ Encourage members to think about their skill and how it can be represented graphically. The designs on the front of their cards should serve as reminders of the skill for the rest of their group.

➔ Tell students how much time they have to finish their cards. As you monitor, nudge the slow workers to speed it up and the quick workers to add more color and visual interest to the front side of the card that will face the other members.

Slide 12

➔ When time is up, ask members to display their cards to their groups.

➔ In turn, have all members show their card and read off the statements on the back.

➔ In return, it's the rest of the group's job to *oohh* and *aahh* and find specific details and phrases to compliment.

➔ If time permits, conduct a quick Gallery Walk where students move as a group to the various other group tables in order to admire their table cards—as well as maybe get ideas for other skills they might use in a discussion.

Slide 13

➔ From this point on, students should display their table cards whenever they are meeting and discussing with their groups.

➔ You can either allow students to keep their cards (if you're pretty certain they will bring them to class every day) or you can collect them.

➔ If you collect them, have students write their names on the inside of the card and have each group nest its cards together. That way you will be able to redistribute the cards quickly the next time groups meet.

Slide 14

➔ And after checking out your groups' skill-inspiring table cards, don't forget to thank each other for their creativity and original work!

LESSON 24: COMPLIMENT CARDS

Why Use It?

Compliment cards offer each group member tangible positive feedback that reinforces behaviors and skills that a student is most likely to bring to the next group.

We love compliment cards because they wrap up so many things in a small package. As you will see, when students write compliment cards they need to reflect on how each person contributed to the group. Plus, members have to craft a short note that shows they've been paying attention to and appreciated those contributions. Think of these cards as a form of thank you notes. Which one would you prefer receiving?

Exhibit A

Thanks for the gift.

Love, Stuart

Exhibit B

Thanks for thinking of me on my birthday. That red and green cardigan Christmas tree sweater is going to be the perfect thing to wear at school in December just before finals begin!

Love, Stuart

Though you may not be in the habit of proffering Christmas sweaters as birthday presents (can you say *regifting?*), Stuart's second note shows *specificity* and *appreciation*, the same qualities we want students to show in their compliment cards.

Compliment cards also serve other functions. They celebrate contributions. They reinforce a classroom community that values gratitude. Compliment cards offer each group member tangible positive feedback that reinforces behaviors and skills that a student is most likely to bring to the next group. Finally, compliment cards offer each member a souvenir of an experience. It's something to keep, put away in a drawer, and accidentally find—and enjoy—years later.

When to Use It

We like to do this lesson after groups have been working together a while or when a group is concluding a cycle and will be disbanding.

Preparation

- This lesson assumes that students have already been working in longer-standing groups of three to five.
- Each student will need an 8 × 5–inch index card.

The Lesson

Slide 1

TITLE: **Compliment Cards**

Slide 2

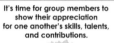

→ Project and read aloud.

Slide 3

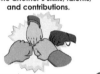

→ Pass out the cards and monitor to make sure everyone has their name at the top of the card.

→ Decide ahead of time whether you'll use first names or full names.

Slide 4

→ Say this:

■ *Now pass your card to the group member to your left; you're passing in a circle. Take a look at the name on the card and think about all the specific contributions that member made to the group.*

Slide 5

→ Project and read instructions aloud.

→ Elaborate:

■ *This is your chance to thank that person for her efforts by writing a compliment.*

■ *Make the compliment as specific as possible.*

■ *Show you really listened to that partner's ideas and noticed the behaviors that really helped the group.*

■ *The compliment can refer to something he did during any of your group's meetings.*

Slide 6

→ Project and read instructions aloud.

→ Elaborate:

  ▪ *Make sure your compliment is positive and will make its recipient feel good.*

  ▪ *This isn't the time to joke around or take a chance on accidentally hurting someone's feelings.*

  ▪ *Remember that this is Home Court.*

→ Typically, if group members have been working together for a while, they're unlikely to write something unfeeling. However, these students are still tweens or teenagers. Enough said. If you aren't feeling 100 percent confident that they'll be kind, tell the class:

  ▪ *This is one of my favorite writing assignments, so after you've finished writing and reading, I'll be collecting the cards so that I can read and enjoy the compliments as well.*

→ As students write, roam the room and monitor. As students finish up, advise:

  ▪ *Just hold tight for a minute while the others catch up, since we'll pass all the cards at one time.*

→ Call time—one more minute—when you want everyone to finish up for passing.

Slide 7

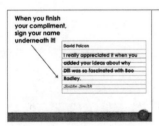

→ Have students legibly sign their full names to their compliments before passing. Full names signify ownership.

→ Always reiterate this step before each pass.

→ After the pass, it's also helpful if you have the next person double-check that the previous writer signed his name.

Slide 8

→ Students pass once again in the same direction.

Slide 9

→ Repeat until the cards get back to the owners.

→ Groups can pass at their own rate, or you can provide a time limit (e.g., two minutes per written compliment) and then announce the next pass.

→ Emphasize that those who finish writing a little earlier than some others should hold on to the cards *until all of them can be passed at once.* Otherwise, you will observe some eager beavers shoving their cards at the next member before they even finished writing on the previous card.

Slide 10

Read your Compliment Cards.

Thank your group members for the compliments and for being great people to work with!

→ Encourage group members to celebrate their successes and the time they've spent together.

Chapter 9

Arguing Agreeably

One of the most advanced forms of small-group interaction is debate—having friendly arguments about sophisticated, challenging, and even divisive topics. As always, we begin by setting a friendly, sociable tone, even as we elicit differing opinions, interpretations, and views from kids. We make sure that students can disagree agreeably, that they have the language to assert different opinions while respecting and honoring each other's thinking. By the end of this unit, kids are able to forcefully advocate for *both sides* of an issue, and then drop controversy to find compromise solutions. We think that's a pretty important life skill for friends, families, workers, and citizens to possess.

LESSON 25: TEXT NUGGETS: FINDING EVIDENCE

Why Use It?

Looking for Text Nuggets requires close reading and rereading, both of which the Common Core emphasizes.

In case you hadn't noticed, the Common Core Standards are obsessed with *arguments using text evidence.* This mandate is manifested, in different ways, in the Reading, Writing, and Speaking and Listening standards. From the standards-writers' standpoint, complete and immutable meaning resides in every text, if only readers can discern the "author's intentions." While we don't fully subscribe to this antique literary theory, that doesn't mean kids shouldn't have to defend their claims with support. Requiring students to bolster their claims with defensible evidence from the text sure does eliminate those crazy kid conversations at the end of a novel that too often swirl around alien abduction.

The starting point for evidence-based argument doesn't need to be formal debates or quasilegal proceedings. What's needed first is practice with careful reading and civilized conversation. Kids need practice backing up their interpretations with text evidence, and we must show them how to notice important details, even while they are reading for the bigger picture.

Looking for Text Nuggets requires close reading and rereading, both of which the Common Core emphasizes. Also, as students discuss their nuggets, it is an opportunity to notice and revisit an author's specific craft choices, which often include how well writers back up their arguments.

When to Use It

This lesson comes first in the argument family because it focuses on careful reading and pleasant discussion. The acrimony can wait for later. The timing depends on your content area and the topic of study at hand. Since its goal is closer reading, this lesson is useful when students are working in literature circles, reading short articles or historical documents, or bringing in passages for discussion. This lesson also helps students examine how a nonfiction author uses evidence to persuade or argue.

Preparation

- Determine how groups will be formed. This lesson works well for pairs or groups of three or four.
- Students should be familiar with at least one method of text annotation.
- Decide on your close-reading goal and choose a short text—about a page—that reflects it. While students will be observing and discussing an author's craft, that craft could connect to storytelling, argument, persuasion, or exposition.
- You will need a copy of the text for each student.

The Lesson

Slide 1

TITLE: **Text Nuggets: Finding Evidence**

Slide 2

→ Pass out the text students will use.

→ Say:

- *In a few minutes, you will read this text silently. As you read, I'm going to ask you to underline phrases or sentences that really jump out at you. When you find them, you'll underline them.*

→ We'll call these phrases or sentences Text Nuggets.

Slide 3

What are Text Nuggets?

- Interesting ideas
- Surprising facts
- Vivid imagery
- Creative language

→ Project slide and read aloud.

→ Model Text Nugget annotation for the first paragraph:

- *I'll do the first paragraph while you watch.*

→ Now, ask students to locate a minimum number of Text Nuggets per page. For a two-page text, we would ask for at least three Text Nuggets per page.

→ As students read, monitor the room.

→ For students who finish in a split second, encourage them to reread or quietly interview them about their sentences. Then, if they can't really explain why they picked them, it will give them a reason to reread.

Slide 4

Leading a Text Nugget Discussion

1. Show where your underlined Text Nugget is and wait for everyone to find it.
2. Read the sentence out loud.
3. Have members reread the sentence.

→ Say:

- *In a moment, you are going to share and discuss your Text Nuggets with your group. First, let's talk about how to do that.*

→ Model the discussion for your students before they begin meeting in their groups. Be explicit in showing them the steps, as follows:

1. Point out where your underlined sentence is and wait for everyone to find it.
2. Read the sentence aloud.
3. Have students reread the sentence.

→ Next slide.

Slide 5

→ Ask for volunteers to respond:

- *What do you have to say about my nugget?*
- *What do you picture?*
- *What words do you like?*
- *What does the sentence make you think about?*
- *Why do you think the author wrote it?*
- *Why do you think I picked it?*

→ Give the class a minute to reread the nugget and think about the different ways to respond, as listed on the slide.

→ Continue modeling, eliciting, and coaxing volunteers to vary their responses.

Slide 6

→ Emphasize that whoever reads a nugget shares last.

→ Model sharing your own ideas last.

Slide 7

→ Project and review:

- *When you move to your groups, remember that:*
  - *Members need to take turns sharing a nugget. If you just shared one, you're not going to share again until everyone else has gone.*
  - *We're working on equal sharing of Text Nuggets and thoughtful responses.*

Slide 8

→ Project and review:

- *Don't forget: the person with the Text Nugget always shares last.*
- *Your group's goal is to keep the discussion going on a Text Nugget versus rushing from one to the next.*
- *Remember, there are lots of different ways you can share an idea about the sentence.*

Slide 9

→ Project and review:

- *If your group is doing a good job thinking and talking about the Text Nuggets each of you shares, you'll have no problem keeping the discussion going until I call time.*

Slide 10

→ In just a minute, kids' groups will discuss the rest of the article. Right now, check to see if students have any questions on the process.

→ Before discussion begins, have each group elect a member to keep track of the steps and make sure the group is following that member's prompts.

→ Ask that these "Process Minders" raise their hands and then let the groups get to work.

→ Leave this slide up so as you monitor you can nudge the Process Minders to make sure the group is following the steps.

→ Though each group has someone in charge of the steps, you'll still need to monitor for members taking turns as they share sentences. Otherwise, there will always be at least one group where one member shares *all* of her nuggets and then the rest of the group tells you, "There's nothing left to share."

Slide 11

→ Monitor and call time when you start to see some groups finishing up.

→ Before beginning the whole-class share, say:

■ *Turn back to your group and pick the Text Nugget that created the best, most interesting discussion. Make sure anyone in your group can do a good job explaining the reasons for your choice. Everyone in your group should be able to describe what you talked about and why that sentence was so interesting.*

→ **Note:** For this kind of sharing, it's important that you randomly pick students to share with the class: this is part of the group's interdependence as well as individual accountability. If you always allow groups to elect a speaker, they will usually choose the kid who is most articulate and who talked the most in the group. Then, when you give groups time to review their discussion, the members will just turn to Jon and say, "Think of something to say when she calls on our group." And Jon will obligingly comply because he *likes* to talk in front of the class. And the rest of the group will breathe a sigh of relief and talk about something unrelated to any of the Text Nuggets!

→ Give groups some time to make sure everyone is prepared to speak.

→ As groups share out, this is your chance to point out some of the author's craft elements you might have been dying to discuss. Once a group has explained, there's nothing wrong with you piggybacking on their ideas. However, it's important that you be just "one more voice" in this discussion versus the single voice of authority.

Slide 12

→ Yep, this "thanking your group" business is super important; that's why it's included at the end of just about every lesson!

LESSON 26: HUMAN CONTINUUM

Why Use It?

This lesson and the next are foundational to students being able to make arguments in writing. The oral rehearsal provides the safe and authentic practice that kids need.

This lesson and the next one (Where Do You Stand?) help students to take and support a position—and to listen thoughtfully to the sometimes opposing ideas of classmates. We enact these "agreeable disagreements" in an energetic and physically active process where kids are making their thinking visible, and being invited to change their position (literally and figuratively) in response to new information. These two structures are foundational to students being able to make arguments in writing. The oral rehearsal provides the safe and authentic practice that kids need to build solid arguments on paper.

When to Use It

This one comes early in the game, when we are moving kids toward increasingly pointed debates and arguments. The playful, physical aspect of the Human Continuum keeps these initial disagreements friendly. The chance to talk with multiple partners who have both similar and different views also helps kids practice patient, respectful listening and diplomatic responding.

Preparation

- Have notecards ready for Step 6.
- Decide where the continuum will extend in your classroom.
- Prelabel the five positions by taping corresponding notecards to the floor.
- Ideally, you want a long span and fairly straight line.
- Temporarily push desks back against the walls to clear the space if needed.
- If you will be using an open, stand-up space often (and you should), it may be worthwhile to teach a minilesson on "how we quickly and quietly move the furniture in our room."

The Lesson

TITLE: **Human Continuum**

➔ Invite a few volunteers to share their recollection of the movie *Jurassic Park*.

➔ Say this:

▪ *The film was made in 1993, and it was meant to be totally fiction. But the science of cloning is moving faster than anyone expected. Several recent articles report that dinosaurs and other extinct animals could soon be recreated using fragments of DNA left in their fossils.*

➔ An interesting wrinkle: since almost no surviving tissues contain complete genetic material, would-be replicators would have to splice in some replacement genes from living animals. The results: Who knows?

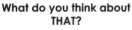

➔ Let kids think quietly or chat with a buddy.

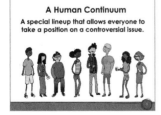

➔ Say:

▪ *In a moment, we are going to form a Human Continuum. This is a special lineup that allows everyone to take a position on a controversial issue and talk to people with similar—and different—outlooks.*

➔ You might ask if anyone has done an activity like this before. There are many iterations, but most people enjoy participating in them.

Slide 6

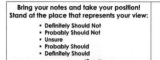

→ Pose the questions on the slide. Say:

- *Take a minute to think about your position. Where will you stand and why?*

→ Make sure kids get some writing down before moving to the next step. You can say:

- *In a minute you'll have to explain your position to several people, so be sure to get your thoughts down.*

Slide 7

→ You'll show this just briefly as kids move into position.

Slide 8

→ **This step needs your very active management.** You want kids to promptly start talking to one (or at most two) other kids standing near them in line.

→ Time to coach!

→ Some may form groups of four or five, where there is very little positive social pressure or airtime for anyone. Some may find it hard to identify a partner.

→ Work up the line, splitting up too-big groups:

- *You are two groups now; continue the conversation.*

→ Put singletons together:

- *This is your partner; talk about your reasons for standing here.*

→ Leave this slide up to support kids as they discuss.

Slide 9

→ Now ask for one volunteer from each section of the line, to get a sense of the various reasons people have for their opinions.

→ If you anticipate that many kids will stand in the middle just to play it safe or make it easier, you can eliminate the "neutral" position and make this a forced choice instead.

Slide 10

→ Now you "fold the line." (This is where the wide-open space is most needed.)

→ The kids at the two extreme ends of the continuum walk until they are facing each other, bringing the continuum with them, and everyone gets a new partner or two.

➔ The fail-safe version: simply take the hand of the kid at one end; have everyone join hands and follow you into position.

➔ The result should be a double line of kids facing each other. Most students will now be facing and talking with someone who *disagrees* with them. (In the middle section, we get less contrast and may need to stir kids around to get new partners.)

➔ We have done this in groups of 250 people, so don't think it is too complicated. Be active, coach like crazy, make it work!

➔ Same discussion rules as before, you want kids *talking in partners or threes only*, and you'll need to police this vigorously.

Slide 11

➔ Again, ask for sampling of the different conversations. This time, you can focus kids' comments on how they were able to disagree agreeably.

➔ If you wish, keep a class list of the successful strategies and language kids used (have a Student Scribe do the listing so you can stay focused on managing the conversation.)

Slide 12

➔ The next few steps happen while kids remain standing.

➔ This is the first of two slides providing more information for kids to think about. The two items on this slide give reasons *not* to clone extinct animals.

➔ Allow a few seconds for students to read (they will see the text again soon, so you don't need to linger).

Slide 13

➔ This gives two reasons why we *should* experiment with cloning. Let kids digest these briefly.

Slide 14

- Think about your position in light of this new information.
- Review your notes and revise them if you need to.
- Decide if you want to change your position.

➔ Now ask the kids if any of these facts make them want to reconsider their position. Or, perhaps, this information strengthens their existing position by providing a new argument:

  ▪ *Whether you change your position or not, you should all be incorporating this new information into your position.*

➔ Leave time for writing notes and put up the next slide.

Slide 15

- Bringing back extinct animals might also bring back ancient viruses, bacteria, or other pathogens that could be dangerous to humans.
- Cloning attempts with living mammals have been plagued with problems. The majority of cloned animals die very quickly, and some have suffered greatly.
- If humans pushed some animals to extinction, maybe it is our responsibility to bring them back if we can.
- Cloning extinct animals might speed up genetic technology and lead to cures for a variety of diseases.

➔ Show the information again for kids' reference as they make notes.

Slide 16

→ Now have kids take up their revised positions in line. You may want to say:

- *You may have changed your position significantly in response to this new information. Or, you may have changed your position just slightly toward one end or the other. Be sure to find your just-right place along the continuum as you talk to others.*

Slide 17

→ The discussion directions for kids' conversations with their partly new neighbors. As you supervise, help kids form new pairs.

Slide 18

→ There are two strands to debrief here:

- The topic: the cloning of extinct animals.
- The process (more important!) of developing and supporting arguments.

→ Again, have someone scribe key learnings or language for future use.

Slide 19

→ *Thank you!*

LESSON 27: WHERE DO YOU STAND?

Why Use It?

Like the Human Continuum, this lesson invites students to take a position, both intellectually and physically. In this version, instead of forming a line, we use the corners of the room (or other workable spaces) for kids to gather according to their stance on an issue. Think of this as a "living Likert Scale"—you know, that survey format where people take positions on a 4- or 5-point range that goes from "strongly agree" to "strongly disagree"? Once assembled, kids' task is to explain and defend their reasoning, first with same-opinion partners, and then with people who disagree.

When to Use It

This provides a great way to quickly build energy and curiosity around questions of value and to set kids up for both oral and written argumentation.

This is part of our sequence of "friendly disagreement" lessons. It starts with a safe conversation with someone with whom you agree, and then moves to respectful debating with students who hold a different view. Once kids learn this structure, we use it all year long, whenever controversial topics come up in a unit we are teaching. It is a great way to quickly build energy and curiosity around questions of value (e.g., colonization, drones, privacy, climate change, genetically modified foods) and to set kids up for both oral and written argumentation.

Preparation

- Determine in advance where the four or five gathering areas will be and label each by hanging a label on the wall.
- If your classroom's corners are cluttered, choose and label other spaces. Sometimes "out in the hall" needs to be one space.
- There is one wrinkle with this lesson: you can't necessarily expect an even distribution of views, so sometimes you need to be able to manage one large group and some much smaller ones.

The Lesson

Slide 1

TITLE: **Where Do You Stand?**

Slide 2

→ Ask kids to mention some of the things people disagree about: politics, religion, sports teams, etc.

Slide 3

→ Say something like this:

- *If we want to win arguments in life—and write good, persuasive essays in school—we have to listen to the other side.*

- *Great arguers don't just make their own points forcefully; they also carefully listen and respond to the other side's claims.*

Slide 4

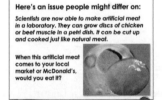

→ Allow some quiet thinking time or informal partner talk.

→ If the *in vitro* meat topic won't work for your kids, feel free to substitute another highly controversial, kid-relevant issue.

Slide 5

→ Allow some think time; then nudge students toward writing.

→ Make sure all kids have some notes down before you turn them loose to take positions.

Slide 6

→ The movement and setup for this should be easy if your kids have done the Human Continuum (Lesson 26). It is the same basic idea: students simply move to a designated location that represents their view.

→ Notice that this one is "forced choice"; there is no "neutral" position.

Slide 7

→ Now kids turn to one or two other students standing in the same spot, and immediately begin sharing their reasons for taking this stand.

→ **This step needs your very active management**. Some kids may drift into *de facto* groups of four or five where there is very little positive social pressure or airtime for anyone. Others may find it hard to identify a partner.

→ Time to coach!

→ Work the corners, splitting up too-big groups:

- *You are two groups now; continue the conversation.*

→ Put singletons together:

- *This is your partner; talk about your reasons for standing here.*

→ Leave this slide up to support kids as they discuss.

→ At this stage they are talking with someone who takes the same position, but it might be helpful to say:

- *Yes, you agree with each other, but your partner might have different and important reasoning, so listen carefully.*

Slide 8

→ Be sure to press kids to enunciate their *reasons* for the position they have taken.

Slide 9

→ There are lots of ways to mix up the groups, including simply asking half the class, as volunteers, to relocate to a different corner. This is another way:

- *In a minute, half of each group will move to a different corner. The half with the earliest birthdays in the year will move, and the half with the later birthdays will stay put.*

→ Manage the migration so that each corner has a balanced assortment of people representing different views, so there can be good arguments in every location.

Slide 10

→ The aim is for "new" arrivals to talk with kids who were already in this corner. We don't want the holdovers talking to each other again.

Slide 11

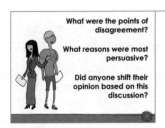

→ Again, ask for volunteers to share from each of the new "mixed opinion" corners.

→ During this debriefing, probe into how opinions might have been swayed or changed during this discussion, and what kind of evidence was most persuasive.

→ Have a Student Scribe list useful ideas or language for future use.

Slide 12

→ Taking a vote is always fun. One of the very intentional side effects of lessons like this one—and using such polarizing topics—is that it can get kids interested in reading nonfiction on their own. Every day there is more information in the news, from patented seeds, to Frankenstein-ian chemical flavor enhancements, to movements for and against genetically modified foods. And those are just questions from the food world!

→ Don't be surprised if your kids bring in more stories or clippings they've found after this lesson!

Slide 13

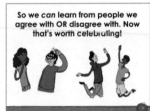

→ Sum it up!

→ *Thanks to all!*

LESSON 28: HEARING EVERYONE'S IDEAS FIRST

Why Use It?

Whenever student groups have choices about how to complete tasks, interpret a text, or organize an argument, members need to remember that Hearing Everyone's Ideas *before* making a decision is important. The result will be a higher-quality final product and also smoother working relationships, because everyone feels their ideas are valued.

When to Use It

Introduce this lesson at the beginning of a group project assignment, when students must decide on a specific project goal and determine what needs to be done to achieve that goal.

The best time to introduce this lesson is at the beginning of a group project assignment, when students must decide on a specific project goal and then determine what needs to be done to achieve that goal. You can embed this lesson right in that project or unit. Teach it at the beginning, and then, as groups work together on the content-specific tasks, you can return to some of these slides for a quick reminder that it's important to hear from everyone in order to make the best decisions.

Preparation

- This lesson assumes that students are already working in groups of three to five.
- Decide how students will record their group's skill notes.

The Lesson

Slide 1

TITLE: **Hearing Everyone's Ideas First**

Slide 2

→ Say something like this:

- *Groups often fail to consider all possible ideas before making a decision. To get the best possible thinking, we need to be sure that everyone contributes and shares equally.*

Slide 3

→ *Sometimes the group members get so focused on completing the task, they just take the first idea that comes along just so they can get started.*

Slide 4

→ *Very often, a group member will have a better idea or a valid concern but never voice it. Therefore, groups need to use discussion skills that enable members to listen to all ideas up front before making any decisions.*

Slide 5

→ Once students understand the importance of listening to every idea before making a decision, have members brainstorm individually first.

→ Their list can include:

- Specific project ideas
- Questions
- Concerns
- Talents members possess
- Other things

➔ The point is that when the group meets, each member has already given the project/task some focused consideration.

Slide 6

➔ *Now that everyone has some solid ideas to share, we want to refine our sharing skills so that each group carefully considers everyone's ideas before making a decision.*

Slide 7

➔ Demonstrate how to fold and label the paper as students follow along. If you have been using this resource all year, they have set up Looks Like/ Sounds Like notes many times!

Slide 8

➔ When you show this slide, emphasize that we are just examining the body language of groups who are Hearing Everyone's Ideas. Don't start them talking yet.

Slide 9

➔ Split groups into pairs for this step.

➔ Though students are working in larger project groups, the brainstorming and discussion of what Hearing Everyone's Ideas Looks Like will go faster if you use pairs at this stage.

➔ Give a few minutes' talk and writing time.

Slide 10

➔ Before the sharing and listing commences, designate a Student Scribe so that you will be free to mingle and monitor as the class shares.

➔ As you call on pairs to contribute to the class master list, be sure to record all the behaviors on the board or, ideally, briefly switch to projectable word processing; that way you'll have a permanent copy of the list.

➔ If you do write directly on the board, take a photo of the finished Looks Like list with your smartphone before you erase.

➜ Instruct students to add new ideas to their Looks Like column so that they have a complete list as well. A typical list will include the following:

- Eye contact
- Focus on the speaker
- Jotting notes
- Smiling
- One person speaks at a time
- Sitting close together
- Focusing on the speaker
- Taking turns speaking
- Nodding in agreement
- Sitting straight
- Leaning in

Slide 11

➜ *Now it's time to talk about what people actually say to each other when they are Hearing Everyone's Ideas.*

➜ *This time we are creating a list of actual phrases you could use when working with others in the classroom.*

Slide 12

➜ Have partners flip their papers over to the right-hand column and label it "Sounds Like."

Slide 13

➜ Create a master list of all the positive phrases students could say to each other. Put each phrase in quotes.

➜ Remind students to write down all of the new ideas so that their personal lists are just as complete as the one on the board.

➜ Typical suggestions include:

- Addressing members by name
- "_____, what are your ideas?"
- "Who has questions?"
- "What else is on your list?"
- "If we choose this project, how would we divide the work?"
- "Which project could best use our unique talents?"

- "Check your lists. Is there anything else that hasn't been contributed?"
- "Let's hear everyone's ideas before we make a decision."
- "What would be the advantages and disadvantages of each of these project ideas?"

Slide 14

➜ Once the T-Chart is complete, pairs should return to their project/task groups and begin discussing their lists of ideas.

➜ Monitor for balanced participation.

➜ Ask questions of groups that appear to be making decisions rather quickly in order to determine how well they've really considered everyone's ideas.

Slide 15

➜ As conversations wind down, encourage groups to review all of the ideas they've discussed and pick the best idea to work with.

➜ Then invite each group to share its intentions with the rest of the class.

➜ After all groups have shared, have students give each other a big round of applause for all the thought that went into their project decisions.

Slide 16

Thank your group for listening and carefully considering your ideas!

➜ Then have the students turn back to their individual groups and thank each other for listening to and carefully considering their ideas.

LESSON 29: ARGUING BOTH SIDES

Why Use It?

Being able to formulate arguments on both sides of an issue helps our students to become better thinkers and—hopefully—better citizens.

Aside from the fact that the Common Core wants kids to be arguing from elementary school up, being able to formulate arguments on both sides of an issue helps our students to become better thinkers and—hopefully—better citizens. Though our various news sources claim to be "fair and balanced," are they? Informed citizens examine arguments and scrutinize evidence for their veracity. Are both sides equally well supported? Sometimes yes, but often no. This lesson helps kids become better persuaders, but also better at seeing both sides of complex issues.

When to Use It

This is the lesson to use whenever you want to teach persuasion and argumentation. Its structure requires that students argue both sides of an issue, and then drop their final positions, pooling all available information in order to generate the best possible solution to the problem posed.

Though this lesson appears a bit complicated, students adapt to it readily. However, we do recommend that you repeat this lesson two or three times, so that students become adept at argumentative maneuvering. Also, don't be afraid to return to this lesson later in the school year, particularly during test prep season. If students clearly understand that developing an argument requires addressing more than just your preferred viewpoint, their essays will score well.

Preparation

- Decide ahead of time how groups of four will form.
- You will need distinct shoulder (side by side) and face partners (partners who are across a table from each other).
- Decide how you want to arrange the furniture so that groups and partners can best focus on each other.
- Insist on tight seating. As students plan and argue, the volume will become distracting unless group members sit close together. You want students to concentrate on their partners, speak quietly, and avoid distractions from other groups.
- Review the Membership Grid (see page 106) warm-up interview. You will be using it in this lesson.

- Have a copy of the Membership Grid form for everyone (page 213 in the Resources and www.corwin.com/teachingsocialskills).

- Pick an issue related to your content area and current unit of study.

- Choose two short pieces of text, about one page in length each, that give information about opposite sides of that same issue.

- Before photocopying the two articles back to back, *mark the number 1 or 2 clearly at the top of each article*. These numbers will be used to reference the opposing positions.

- Each student will need a copy of both articles (back to back) in order to annotate and research their positions.

The Lesson

Slide 1

TITLE: **Arguing Both Sides**

Slide 2

→ Help kids identify face partners.

Slide 3

→ . . . and shoulder partners.

→ Scan for correct seating arrangement and request necessary adjustments.

Slide 4

→ Once groups are formed, have members start by introducing themselves with their name and a quick, fun factoid: "Hi, I'm Nancy, and my favorite food is guacamole."

→ If kids know each other well, give them a quick trivia question to answer (best TV show, favorite pizza topping, etc.).

Slide 5

→ Distribute forms and follow these brief introductions with a Membership Grid warm-up interview.

→ You may assign a topic, or each group can think of one.

→ Tell groups to spend about one minute interviewing each member.

→ Remind members to listen carefully so that they can ask good follow-up questions.

Slide 6

→ When Membership Grid is done, show this.

Slide 7

→ Avoid confusion by asking one set of face partners to volunteer their birthdays and then demonstrating the math on the board.

→ Afterward, quickly circulate the room and make sure all of the face partners have their number calculated.

Slide 8

→ Ask the face partner pairs with the lowest number in their group to raise their hands. They will be Position 1.

→ Then have the remaining pairs, those with the higher number, raise their hands. They will be Position 2.

→ Circulate once again and double-check that all face partners know whether they are designated a Position 1 or a Position 2.

→ Answer questions as they arise. Of course, students are going to ask about the topic. Assure them—with an air of mystery—that it will be revealed shortly!

Slide 9

→ Announce the topic and pass out the research text. Be sure that all pairs have turned to the correct article:

▪ *If you are Position 1s, you will read and annotate the text marked with a 1. If you are Position 2s, you will read and annotate the text marked with a 2.*

→ Ask if there are any questions and do a quick scan to make sure all the face partner pairs have turned to the correct article for their position.

→ Tell preparation pairs (face partners):

▪ *As you read, mark information that makes or supports an argument for your side.*

→ Give students some silent time to read individually.

Slide 10

→ As the preparation pairs (face partners) finish up their reading, tell them to convene and plan their arguments.

→ Indicate how many minutes (we typically give 5–7 minutes) they have to plan. Circulate, and observe the work.

→ If pairs finish earlier and it appears they have good arguments, call time early. Likewise, if more time is needed, give groups a few more minutes.

Slide 11

→ Have groups recheck their seating position and reacquaint themselves with their *shoulder* partners, with whom they will be arguing momentarily.

Slide 12

→ Beforehand, decide how many minutes you will give each side to argue.

→ When students argue for the first time, we like to keep things short and give each side only a minute. When students become more skilled, you can give each side two minutes. However, it's important to keep this activity moving briskly.

→ Remind the students:

- *You can only listen while your partner is arguing. However, taking notes on your partner's arguments will be useful later, so I highly recommend that you do so!*

→ Make sure all pairs are ready and in argument position; then signal the start of the argument round by yelling, "Go!"

Slide 13

→ Call time using your Quiet Signal (from page 64). Wait for arguing to end.

→ Remind the "new" listeners that the same rules apply: listen silently and take notes.

→ Make sure opponents are ready and then signal for the arguing to begin.

Slide 14

Prepare Refutation

What is the other side's weakest argument?
Locate new proof or tough questions.

→ Call time again using your Quiet Signal.

→ Tell students to refocus attention on their preparation pairs (face partners):

- *Having both heard the opposition's best arguments, your job now is to work together to poke holes in those arguments so that you can later attempt to persuade your argument partners to change their viewpoint.*

- *One of the best ways to knock holes in an opponent's assumptions is to ask for specific examples and details or ask pointed questions. You can ask your opponent for evidence from the text.*

→ If students still seem unsure of how to plan their refutation, take a moment to model from a topic different from the one students are presently arguing. Pick a topic from your own school culture with which students are familiar. Here's an example:

- *There's some debate over whether everyone should have a full period for lunch; right now only juniors and seniors do. Here's one side of the argument. I want you to listen closely and think about how you can prove me wrong, knock holes in my thinking.*

- *Instead of expanding lunchtime for everyone, I think we should return to the days when everyone only had half a period to eat.*

- *First, now that our enrollment is down, it shouldn't be a problem for anyone to buy food and eat in twenty-five minutes. The cafeteria was redesigned during remodeling. There are now more food stations as well as cashiers. Plus, if no one had a full period for lunch, there would be plenty of seats.*

- *Second, students could use the other half of the period to get academic help or complete homework. They could use the media center; they could attend one of the various resource centers; they could stay in their assigned homerooms and complete homework.*

- *Okay, turn to your face partner and figure out some ways you can refute my arguments for having shorter lunch periods. Remember, your goal is to reveal my arguments' weak points. What is inaccurate? What did I forget to mention? What questions do you have that I did not answer?*

→ Give students a few minutes to talk with their face partners and jot some notes; then take responses. If you feel it would enhance your students' understanding, assign a Student Scribe to list the responses on the board so that students can refer to them as they plan their own refutation that they will soon use with their argument partners.

→ Possible "lunch period" refutation ideas might include:

- Students need some time to relax during lunch versus rushing to buy and eat their food in half a period.

- Eating food quickly is unhealthy. Plus, when students are rushed, they tend to buy food that can be eaten quickly, which is usually junk food. You can eat french fries a lot quicker than you can chew a salad.

- What evidence do you have that providing everyone with a homeroom/resource time will improve student achievement?

→ After moving through this example, ask if there are any questions. Then instruct students to turn back to their face partners and plan the refutation they will present to their argument partners.

→ Monitor the pairs as they work, encouraging them to really dig into a weak argument.

→ As you see groups finishing up (about five minutes), call time.

Slide 15

Rules for Civilized Refutation

1. Listen carefully, whether you agree or not.
2. Criticize ideas, not people.
3. Ask clarification questions.
4. Answer a question with specific examples or evidence from the text.

→ Project and read aloud Rules for Civilized Refutation.

→ Then say:

- *When you meet again with your argument partner, your discussion can focus only on the arguments. Criticizing the person is not allowed.*

Slide 16

Time to refute!

Turn to your shoulder partner who has the opposite position.

- Point out the weakest argument and explain why.
- Ask tough questions.
- Opponent can respond!!

→ Project and read aloud.

→ Ask if there are any questions.

➔ Announce which number will begin and how many minutes each refutation round will have.

➔ Once again, pairs will take turns with their argument partners as they attempt to refute their opponent's weakest point.

➔ *However,* the big difference is that this time both partners can inject an idea, ask questions, or give answers.

➔ Emphasize that students need to still treat this "debate" as an opportunity to learn and understand. You should observe rational discussions versus interrupting and stonewalling.

Slide 17

➔ Call time. Now the other side takes the lead in questioning the opponent.

Slide 18

➔ The conclusion of the argument is a repeat of the initial steps. But now, *students are going to trade positions.*

➔ Depending on the time available, you may:

- Have students go directly into arguing their new positions using the notes they took during the initial argument rounds.

- Or, if time permits, have students return to their preparation partners in order to discuss their notes and text as they prepare for arguing their new positions.

Slide 19

➔ Tell the students:

- *The same rules apply as in the first argument rounds.*

- *If you are not arguing, then you are silently listening. No interrupting.*

➔ Use the same timing as you did for Slides 11 through 13.

Slide 20

➔ Call time and switch.

Slide 21

→ Call time again.

→ Project and read aloud. Explain:

- *Now your goal is different. Rather than trying your best to defend and argue your position, your goal with your shoulder partner is to come up with the best possible solution to the problem under discussion.*

- *Using the best information from both sides, find the most promising solution. This might mean agreeing with one side or the other, finding a compromise that incorporates the best ideas of both sides, or maybe even coming up with a brand-new solution that neither side considered.*

→ Give pairs a few minutes to work as you monitor.

→ When you call time, have each pair quickly share their solution. Your class will be surprised by the many different, creative, and feasible solutions presented.

Slide 22

→ Celebrate the hard work of the preparation partners and the argument partners.

→ Student pairs should address each other by name and thank each other for the help and the arguments. It also never hurts to lead the entire class in a big round of applause.

Further Comments

An even easier way to jump into this argument model is to eliminate the reading and annotating by picking a topic that your students can argue instinctively. Here are two of our favorite topics:

- Homework should/should not be assigned.
- When I get my driver's license, I should/should not get my own car.

As students become more practiced in the argument structure, have them reflect on how well they are digging deeply into the material you provide in order to develop strong arguments as well as challenge the ideas of their opponent. Are they using evidence from the text to support their arguments?

The more sophisticated students become in developing oral arguments, the more fluid and solid their written arguments will become. We think that any persuasive or argumentative writing task should be preceded by a chance to work on the ideas out loud, with others.

LESSON 30: CIVILIZED DISAGREEMENT

Why Use It?

This lesson reinforces the need for kids to bring evidence to arguments. It also teaches students that disagreements can be civilized.

As we are well aware, posing a good argument, in speaking and writing, is a cornerstone of the Common Core and many state standards. However, these standards also explicitly state that argument is to be of an academic, rational, evidence-based nature, not a screamfest. The use of emotional appeals is frowned upon (though they often work quite well in real life). This lesson offers you the opportunity to reinforce the need for kids to bring evidence, not just loud voices, to an argument.

When to Use It

The more adept students become at using the argument model in Lesson 29, the bolder they will become—and the greater the likelihood that they will try to pick up a few moves from the talking heads on those cable news shows.

Flip through the twenty-four hour news networks and almost any time of day you're bound to catch some really bad arguing taking place. This includes but is not limited to name calling, interrupting, smirking, eye-rolling, blatantly ignoring the other person's ideas, or injecting ideology over fact.

While some viewers may find this entertaining, *ad hominem* behavior in the classroom shuts down thinking and creates a bad feeling. Therefore, it's important for students to understand that disagreement can take place in a civilized way that allows both parties to learn—and maybe even change their minds when presented with logical arguments supported by strong facts and examples!

Preparation

- This lesson is best executed with partners, so decide ahead of time how kids will pair up.
- You also need to decide how students will record their skill notes.

The Lesson

Slide 1

TITLE: **Civilized Disagreement**

Slide 2

→ Begin by reminding students of Home Court:

- *We're all here to learn from each other and help each other do our very best.*

Slide 3

→ *So when we argue, it's okay to disagree with each other. As a matter of fact, it's expected!*

→ *But even when we disagree, we still need to remember Home Court. That means treating others respectfully and viewing every opportunity to argue as an opportunity to learn.*

→ *When we argue, the goal is not to "win at all costs"—though you might see people on television behave this way.*

Slide 4

→ *Have you ever listened to political talk radio or watched Fox, CNN, MSNBC, or any of the Sunday talk shows? Have you ever watched* Real Time With Bill Maher?

→ *Have you noticed that guests argue quite a bit on these shows but seldom seem persuaded by or even listen to the other side?*

→ *What do they do instead?*

→ **Note:** Depending on your students' background knowledge you might think about finding a quick YouTube of one of these television programs to show them here. Of course, preview it first!

→ Ask them:

- *What does uncivilized argument look like? What does it sound like?*

- *Turn to your partner and discuss what these "arguers" look like and sound like. What body language do you notice? What do they say to each other?*

→ When they are done discussing, ask pairs to share. Just listen to their observations; do not write them down. Students will likely describe some of the following:

Uncivilized Argument

Body Language	What People Say
Rolling eyes	Sighing
Shaking head	Interrupting
Arms crossed	"You don't know . . ."
Aggressive finger pointing	Citing emotions, ethics, religion
Leaning back	Shouting
Looking at the person as if he's crazy	"You're wrong!"
Looking bored, tired	"You don't know what you're talking about!"
Pounding fist	"That is not true!"
Waving someone off—dismissive gesture	"That's a stupid idea!"

Slide 5

→ Make the point that we don't want to argue this way.

→ *We want to learn from each other and respect each other. We want to disagree with ideas intelligently versus attack the person who presented them.*

→ *Now, how would we need to behave in order to make that happen?*

→ *How can we challenge a partner's ideas without attacking that person personally?*

Slide 6

→ Demonstrate how to fold and label the paper as students follow along.

Slide 7

→ When you show this slide, emphasize that we are just examining the *body language* of pairs who are participating in civilized disagreement. What does it *look* like?

Slide 8

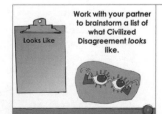

→ Monitor groups as they jot down their body language descriptors.

→ Remind groups to focus on positive behaviors.

Slide 9

→ Before the sharing and listing commences, designate a Student Scribe so that you will be free to mingle, monitor, and coach as the class shares.

→ As you call on pairs to contribute to the class master list, record all the behaviors on the board or, ideally, briefly switch to projectable word processing; that way, you'll have a permanent copy of the list.

→ If you write directly on the board, take a photo of the finished Looks Like list with your smartphone before you erase.

→ Instruct students to add new ideas to their Looks Like column so that they have a complete list as well.

→ A typical list will include:

- Eye contact
- Focused attention
- Looking interested
- Nodding head
- Smiling, friendliness
- Taking notes
- Taking turns
- Waiting until a speaker's time is up before talking

Slide 10

→ *Now it's time to talk about what people actually say to each other when they are participating in civilized disagreement.*

→ *This time we are creating a list of actual phrases you could use when working with others in the classroom.*

Slide 11

→ Have partners flip their papers over to the right-hand column and label it "Sounds Like."

Slide 12

→ Create a master list of all the positive phrases students could say in order to disagree civilly with each other.

→ Put each phrase in quotes.

➜ Remind students to write down all of the new ideas so that their personal lists are just as complete as the one on the board.

➜ Typical suggestions include:

- "What makes you feel that you are right?"
- "Why do you think that?"
- "What evidence/examples/facts lead you to believe this?"
- "Where did you find this in the text?"
- "Give us some support for this idea."
- "I disagree. What about the instance in which . . . ?"
- "Have you ever considered . . . ?"
- "What if . . . ?"

Slide 13

➜ Compare this skill chart with their initial observations about uncivilized argument.

➜ *What differences do you notice?*

Slide 14

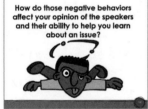

➜ *How might the argument partners feel after an uncivilized argument versus a civilized one? Which style might actually be more persuasive? Why?*

Slide 15

➜ End by having partners thank each other and reassure each other that arguing with them is always going to be a pleasure and a learning experience.

Slide 16

➜ And that you might even change your mind if logically persuaded!

Chapter 10

Small-Group Projects

As students develop all these families of social-academic skills, they become increasingly capable of pursuing larger, longer-term tasks with less direct teacher control. As teams, they can take responsibility for their choices and decisions, setting goals and timetables, keeping records, and monitoring their own progress. In terms of the gradual release of responsibility model, this is the final stage—independent practice—where the teachers withdraw direct supervision and decision making, and now serve as advisers and coaches to trustworthy learners.

We recommend that you teach Lessons 31, 32, and 33 together as the start-up to your first long-term, small-group inquiry project of the year.

Lesson 31. Developing an Assessment Rubric

Lesson 32. Planning Group Projects

Lesson 33. Keeping Individual Project Logs

Lesson 34. Midcourse Corrections

Lesson 35. Being an Attentive Audience Member

LESSON 31: DEVELOPING AN ASSESSMENT RUBRIC

Why Use It?

Students are most likely to aim for high quality when *they* design the rubric along with you.

When kids are starting an ambitious, extended group project, it is very helpful for them to know where they are going. What are the goals, the outcomes, the learnings, the achievements that the group aims to accomplish? How will kids know when they have done great work? When the project is done, what elements of the work should be assessed or graded?

Rubrics have definitely become the go-to assessment tool for complex, long-term work. However, most of the time these rubrics come from somewhere else: the teacher, the district, the College Board, and so on. What a missed opportunity! Students are most likely to aim for high quality when *they* design the rubric along with you. Typically, when we hand ready-made rubrics to kids, they ignore them until the grade has been determined. But if students co-create the official assessment tool for a product or performance, they're the ones who must grapple with the Big Question: What does high quality look like?

We want to stress that in creating a scoring rubric at the start of a project, we aren't trying to constrain kids' creativity or prematurely lock them into criteria that might later prove irrelevant. There are certain kinds of recurrent group projects, like book clubs, where the structure is quite predictable and we can accurately describe in advance what a high-quality performance should look like. With more open-ended research projects, such as inquiry circles, we may have to adjust the initial rubric as kids' research unfolds.

When to Use It

This lesson shows students how to examine a product, pinpoint key components, and then create attributes that help define a high-quality outcome. We recommend spreading this lesson over two days. On the first day, create the Pizza Rubric. On the second day, create a rubric for the class assignment/project at hand.

Preparation

- Decide ahead of time how partners will pair up.
- Duplicate the Pizza Rubric handout (page 215) and the blank Project Rubric (page 216 in the Resources and www.corwin.com/teachingsocialskills) back to back.
- Be prepared to project a blank pizza rubric that can be filled in by the class—or have one ready on the board (Slide 7).
- You may want to have examples of rubrics for your class to examine (Slide 8).
- Be prepared to project a more general blank rubric that can be filled in by the class—or have one ready on the board (Slide 9).

The Lesson

Day 1

Slide 1

TITLE: **Developing an Assessment Rubric**

Slide 2

→ Say something like this:

- *When you are starting on a project, it's good to figure out ahead of time how to make it "high quality." Usually, the quality of a project is measured against a rubric.*

Slide 3

→ *In order to give us some practice thinking about how to define quality, we're going to start by talking about pizza.*

→ *Turn to your partner and conduct an interview about pizza. You might ask which toppings are favorites, the best place to get pizza, whether thin or thick crust is better, or what was the worst pizza your partner ever had.*

→ *You'll probably think of other questions as well. Go ahead and get started.*

→ Give pairs a couple of minutes to talk, and then continue.

Slide 4

→ Say something like this:

- *A rubric defines quality by carefully specifying each of the elements of a successful product or outcome.*

- *Having such a rubric enables someone making a product to shoot for excellence because that person has a concrete understanding of what excellence looks like.*

→ If you have an extra five minutes, cue up this YouTube video: Domino's® Pizza Turnaround. It's the commercial where Domino's admits its pizza is terrible and now is trying to make it better.

→ This is why groups need to think about quality *before* they start, versus after the fact, when it is too late.

Slide 5

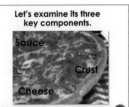

→ *In order to understand how to construct a rubric, let's practice by thinking about pizza quality. Start by considering the three main components of a cheese pizza: crust, sauce, and cheese.*

Slide 6

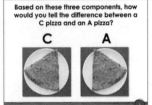

→ *If you were to give cheese pizzas letter grades, what would be the differences between one that got an A and one that got a C?*

Slide 7

→ Pass out copies of the rubric.

→ Explain:

- *Before quality can be defined, we need to think about each product component and figure out the component's underlying attributes. In the case of pizza, the attributes are texture, flavor, and color. Those are the things we need to think about as we define quality for crust, sauce, and cheese.*

Slide 8

→ Say:

- *The order of the grades on the rubric is listed from C to A for a reason. That's because when we examine quality, a product has to meet some minimal requirements in order to be acceptable; that's a C.*

- *To reach a B or an A, those minimal requirements must remain intact while other refinements increase the quality.*

→ Give partners a few minutes to discuss descriptors related to pizza quality and fill in their rubrics.

→ Monitor and read over their shoulders.

→ Intervene when you notice vague descriptors. Help by asking questions that will enable pairs to think about quality in more specific terms.

→ Once all pairs have some ideas for each component and letter grade, select a Student Scribe and create a master rubric.

→ As in past lessons, use a projector or write on the board (this time, filling in a blank pizza rubric) so that students can copy down the descriptors they missed.

→ A finished class pizza rubric might look something like the one on page 191.

→ After finishing the chart, ask:

- *Was it easy or difficult for you to come up with these descriptors?*

- *What items did you consider but decide not to write down?*

- *How did you figure out the difference between an A and B component?*

- *On what descriptors did you and your partner disagree?*

Components	C	B	A
Crust: Texture, flavor, color	Cooked through Pale Neutral flavor	Crisp Light golden Salty	Crunchy Golden brown Buttery
Sauce: Texture, flavor, color	Red Tomato flavor Evenly spread	Medium consistency Spicy	Smooth Fresh tasting
Cheese: Texture, flavor, color	White Bland Mozzarella	Evenly melted Stays on pizza	Chewy Fresh tasting

→ One of the things you—and the class—should notice is that creating a descriptive rubric is *hard*. While it's fairly easy to show a difference between a C and A product, finding suitable descriptors to separate a B from an A is much more difficult.

→ Also, any time you talk about quality, people's own preferences and experiences come into play. There really is no such thing as a completely objective rubric.

→ One other rubric consideration: it's much easier to develop and use a rubric that is restricted to the three *most* important components. Yes, we know that most rubrics have many more categories, but think about it—do more categories create better products? Our goal is for students to examine quality and internalize it. Making a rubric long and complicated hinders this process.

Day 2

Slide 9

→ The following day, have students turn over their pizza rubric and use the back side to design a rubric for an upcoming class assignment.

→ Examine samples (if you have them from previous classes) or collectively imagine (if this is a brand-new assignment) what a great product would look like.

→ Determine what would be the three most important components for this particular assignment. Flip back to the pizza rubric from the previous day. The three most important components for pizza were crust, sauce, and cheese.

→ Ask:

▪ *What would be the three most important components for this assignment?*

Slide 10

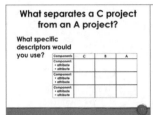

→ Once the components are established, have pairs determine the main attributes of each component.

→ Then, as a class, discuss and agree on two or three attributes for each component. Write these down in each component box on the rubric form.

Slide 11

→ Now pairs begin discussion of the component descriptors. Remind them that a C establishes the minimum threshold of acceptability. B and A descriptors demonstrate additional details and refinement. As they did for the pizza, pairs should try to make the descriptors as specific as possible.

→ Once all pairs have some ideas for each component and letter grade, select a Student Scribe and create a master rubric for the project.

→ As in past lessons, use projection or write on the board so that students can copy down the descriptors they missed. Remember to keep a copy of the rubric (electronic, photo, etc.) so that you can return to it as needed.

Slide 12

→ As students start work on their projects, they should use the class master rubric for guidance. Beginning with the end product in mind will result in fewer missteps and a better focus on how to achieve a high-quality result.

→ When the projects are completed, this is the rubric that you and the class can adapt for assessing the final products.

Slide 13

→ Have groups congratulate and thank each other for the hard work it took to create the rubric.

Further Comments

Remember to collect samples of work that reflect different levels of quality. Physically examining previous models almost always leads to improvement and refinement the following year.

LESSON 32: PLANNING GROUP PROJECTS

Why Use It?

Inquiry projects must be very carefully organized for kids to receive the maximum benefit.

As we mentioned way back in Chapter 2, there's tons of research showing that extended inquiry projects raise kids' achievement and effectively prepare them for many high-stakes tests. In fact, Smokey and our colleague Stephanie Harvey have written a whole book about these "inquiry circles" (2009). But it's less often emphasized that these projects, especially when they are conducted in small groups, must be very carefully organized for students to receive the maximum benefit.

This is the second in a family of lessons designed to provide just that structure—not by handing out the customary term paper list of specifications, warnings, and timelines, but by helping kids take responsibility for themselves. They've already made a rubric specifying what high-quality outcomes for this project would look like (Lesson 31). Now it's time to begin planning the practical steps and stages that will help kids eventually achieve their rubric goals.

When to Use It

This lesson comes after kids have been actively exploring possible topics, rather than at the very start of a research unit. When kids have marinated thoroughly in the subject matter, generated some curiosity, and are homing in on their group topic (and their individual specialties within it), that's when we start the formal planning process.

This is one of the longest social-academic lessons we teach all year. It can sometimes occupy a whole class period, or you can split it into smaller chunks of two days, doing Group Plans on day one and Individual Member Plans the next day.

Preparation

- Make a calendar and copy the two Work Plan forms; print the two-page Group Work Plan Form back-to-back if possible (see pages 217–219 in the Resources and www.corwin.com/teachingsocialskills).

- Prepare to fill in calendar dates with your students *or* fill in key dates before copying the calendar handout (see Slide 3).

- If kids are using research logs, journals, or folders (see Lesson 33) they should have them at the ready.

The Lesson

TITLE: **Planning Group Projects**

→ Say something like this:

- *We are just getting started with our small-group inquiry projects. You have done some preliminary research and chosen your general group topics.*

- *These investigations will be more fun and interesting if you do some careful planning up front—and all along the way.*

→ If you want some conversation around the topic, you could ask kids:

- *What makes research projects hard? What problems have you run into in the past?*

→ Tie their comments back to the idea that being *highly organized* is a strong defense against distraction and despair during extended research projects.

→ Pass out copies of the calendars.

→ Say something like this:

- *Let's begin with a calendar. We can use this to think about:*
  - *When you'll start and end*
  - *What else we have to schedule around*
  - *When would be sensible deadlines*
  - *Dates for the final sharing*
- *Let's get started by working on our own copies of the calendar.*

→ Personalize this with your own goals and timetable for the particular project. You can do it one of two ways:

- **Baseline version:** Fill out the calendar in real time, along with the kids.
- **Time-saver version:** Hand out a calendar with some landmark dates already entered:
  - Start date
  - End date
  - Days for class sharing of findings
  - Days with conflicting activities marked off

And so forth. Either way, the idea is to get kids thinking about the span of time available and how they will manage it.

Slide 4

→ Pass out the Group Work Plan form.

Slide 5

→ Pass out the Individual Group Member Work Plan form.

Slide 6

→ Say something like this:

- *Now take a look at the Work Plan forms I have passed out. There's a two-page form for each group, and a one-page form for each individual group member. Take a look at these.*

→ Let kids quietly read the Work Plan forms.

Slide 7

→ Say something like this:

- *Successful inquiry projects require both* individual *and* group *effort, with tangible outcomes for each.*

- *So you need to specify exactly what each of your groups' members will be doing on their own, and how you will work collaboratively to combine your learning and share it with others.*

→ **Note:** The big point here is the principle of *individual and group accountability.* Each member will complete a portion of the larger investigation, for which that person is accountable to the group and to the teacher. But each group also supports each other along the way, and later, creates a team performance that highlights the group's overall learning. Thus, group accountability. We need both kinds of responsibility for small-group projects to work.

Slide 8

→ *Let's begin with the Group Plan.*

→ Talk students through the Group Work Plan form displayed here and see if they have any questions.

Slide 9

→ Say something like this:

- *Working with your team, talk over your plans and fill out the Group Work Plan form.*

- *We know that new information, hot leads, and schedule changes will pop up along the way. That's why we'll do "Midcourse Corrections" using these forms as the project unfolds.*

→ Allow groups to meet now and make some notes on their Group Work Plan form.

→ This may take ten minutes or more, as you circulate and support groups.

→ Be especially attentive to the way kids are splitting the overall topic into individual subtopics—these need to be substantial and balanced, so that every member is challenged and engaged.

→ Kids probably won't complete this form on the first attempt, and you will encourage them to make clarifications, corrections, and revisions with each successive meeting.

Slide 10

→ Invite some discussion about the process.

→ Then, if they need a few more minutes, send them back to work.

→ When time is running out, make a big deal about the kids' ceremonial signatures. The metaphor of making a contract with one another and with you invests this planning process with a more binding feeling.

→ Have them hand the forms in to you to approve (and copy for your later use).

Slide 11

→ *Let's work on the other form now.*

→ Talk students through the Individual Group Member Work form displayed here and see if they have any questions.

Slide 12

→ Say something like this:

- *Now, working on your own, think about your personal part of the project—your own subtopic or inquiry question.*

- *Fill out the Individual Group Member Work Plan form based on the information you have today.*

- *We know that new information, hot leads, and schedule changes will pop up along the way.*

        ▪   *That's why you'll keep revising and revisiting this form.*

→ Provide some quiet work time with your support.

Slide 13

→ Invite some discussion about the process.

→ If they need a few more minutes, send them back to work.

→ Have kids sign and hand in the forms to you to approve (and copy for your later use).

Slide 14

→ *A final organizational tip: keep everything related to your research in one place!*

→ *Don't worry. Research logs are coming up next!*

LESSON 33: KEEPING INDIVIDUAL PROJECT LOGS

Why Use It?

Recording meeting activities, successes, goals, and responsibilities is an excellent way to keep all group project members involved and accountable.

Accountability can be one of the biggest problems with extended group research projects and with ongoing structures like book clubs or literature circles. Members see that their meeting quality is suffering, or that some members are doing too much—and others too little—and feel helpless to solve the problem. Recording meeting activities and successes as well as goals and responsibilities is an excellent way to keep all members involved and accountable. Also, the log comes in handy when the project is due and each kid has to document his or her contributions to the group and the final product.

When to Use It

The logical time to introduce Project Logs is near the beginning of the year's first substantial group project. Then, each time these groups meet, you can build time into the day's agenda for members to review their last meeting's accomplishments; set goals for the current meeting; and, finally, determine who will take responsibility for each task that needs to be accomplished before the next meeting.

This lesson happens in several shorter segments, with kids doing small-group task work between its stages. It may even stretch across a couple of days, depending on how much work the groups have to tackle.

Preparation

If you have already taught the two previous lessons:

- Kids should have the following tools out on the table whenever they are making Project Log entries. These materials can help them keep close track of individual decisions and group tasks, keeping the pace and quality of work high.
  - Assessment Rubrics (Lesson 31)
  - Work Plans and Calendars (Lesson 32)
- Decide what kinds of logs you want kids to keep—composition book, spiral, or otherwise. Make sure students have access to them during the lesson.
- A stamp and stamp pad are handy to quickly check-in log entries.

The Lesson

Slide 1

TITLE: **Keeping Individual Project Logs**

Slide 2

→ Say something like this:

▪ *A group's project logs are a record of their work.*

Slide 3

→ *Project logs help keep a group organized and on task because the members are always working from a plan or agenda they've negotiated together.*

Slide 4

→ Project and read aloud.

Slide 5

→ *A log clarifies who has to do which tasks and makes everyone accountable to the group, which helps prevent . . .*

Slide 6

→ *. . . misunderstandings.*

Slide 7

→ This slide begins a series of steps where kids will start making entries in their new log. Tell students that everyone should record these steps in their log, so they will have them to refer to at each meeting.

→ **Step 1: Record the date and members present.** Say something like this:

- *Your log will document the accomplishments of the group and each individual. Groups make log entries at the beginning and end of each meeting in order to collect this information.*

- *The first step is to record the date and the members present. Do that now.*

→ Monitor to make sure everyone is correctly beginning the first entry.

→ If you intend to collect the completed logs along with the groups' final product, now is the time to say so.

Slide 8

→ **Step 2: Note any absences.** Read the slide and have groups do this now.

→ Check in with the groups that have absent members and make sure they've assigned someone to bring the missing member up to speed.

→ **Note:** At the first meeting, it's important that group members trade some contact information such as cell phone number or e-mail address (totally old school); therefore, if a member is absent, someone can contact them. Often, absent students will say, "But I was absent," as they try to absolve themselves of responsibility. Groups need to understand that responsibility is a two-way street. It's their duty to keep in contact with absent members, and it's the responsibility of absent members not to make excuses but show up with the work the group needs to continue.

Slide 9

→ **Step 3: Set task goals for the upcoming meeting.** Read the slide and have groups do this now.

→ Once students have determined their goals for their meeting, they are free to get down to business, since the rest of the day's entry will be completed later, at the end of the meeting.

→ Until groups need to view the remaining slides, we recommend that you turn your LCD projector off to save your bulb!

After Group Meetings

Slide 10

→ Tell students they need to record the following steps that they will take after each group meeting. The first three are Log Entries they will make with their *group.* Have them list these steps under the heading Group Reflections.

→ **Step 1: Review your project meeting goals for today.** Read the slide and have them review their task goals and check-off those they completed.

→ As groups review what they accomplished in their meeting, monitor the conversations.

Slide 11

→ **Step 2: Make a list of what you need to accomplish.** Read the slide aloud and have them work together on their lists.

→ When they are finishing up their lists, say something like this:

▪ *Now, assign important tasks to each group member. Your goal is to establish fairness and equality. That means everyone shoulders the project burden evenly. No one should walk away without a responsibility, and no one should walk away feeling like they're the one who has to do everything!*

→ As you monitor the task assignments, look for groups talking in specific terms rather than making vague, general statements. If you hear the latter, stop and ask members to describe the tasks in more specific terms. For example, what does "finding costumes" mean? Does it mean that each person is going to go through the family closet? Visit a thrift store? What are these costumes going to look like? When students make plans, they need to be specific or misunderstandings and frustration can result.

Slide 12

→ **Step 3: Review who will contact missing group members.** Read the slide aloud and have them do this quick step, to remind kids what they committed to do earlier.

→ Remind them:

▪ *This step is in everyone's interest—just because a member is absent, it doesn't mean that person doesn't have to do any work in between this meeting and the next one!*

Slide 13

→ Now kids switch from making *group-related* entries to *individual* reflections. Have them list these three steps under the heading Individual Reflections.

→ **Step 1: List your specific contributions to today's meeting.** Read the slide and have them write their list.

→ Encourage all members to list in detail *all* of the contributions they made in today's meeting. Insist that they be specific. Writing down, "I gave ideas" gives no real information. Writing down, "I suggested we meet this Saturday in the Ryerson Research Library at the Art Institute; it has a great collection of fashion magazines from the Civil War era that would help with our costume design" shows some real thinking.

Slide 14

→ **Step 2: Make a plan for completing your responsibilities.** Read the slide and say something like this:

▪ *I want you to each review your responsibilities to the group. What do you need to accomplish before the next meeting? As before, be specific in your plans. This is the key to getting the job done well and enhancing the next group meeting.*

→ If kids are using a Project Assessment Rubric, be sure to emphasize that any project planning should be directly connected to the rubric.

→ Continue monitoring for specificity as well as giving a hand to those who need your assistance or advice.

Slide 15

→ **Step 3: What can you do next time to improve the group's meeting?** Read the slide and say something like this:

- *Finally, I want each of you to consider how you might improve your next meeting:*
  - *Do you need to come better prepared?*
  - *Participate more actively?*
  - *Ask more questions?*
  - *Talk less?*
  - *Keep everyone involved?*
- *It's important for everyone to remember that your behaviors affect others.*

→ Have them make explicit notes. Monitor, again, and make sure they have something specific that they plan to improve.

→ Highly recommended: check-in the entries as each meeting adjourns. This is easy to do as you monitor the room.

→ Stop at each student's desk, give a quick skim, and put a stamp in the margin.

→ **Note:** Without check-ins, students might try to complete their log entries the night before the project is due or not complete the entries at all. Both actions defeat the purposes just described in the earlier slides.

Slide 16

→ Before a meeting ends, members need to talk together to confirm their individual responsibilities and discuss the when, where, and how of getting the job done.

→ Members should also talk about what group skills they are using well and what each member could do better the next time.

→ If time permits, ask each group to give a quick report to the rest of the class on what members plan to accomplish before the next meeting. Sharing plans publicly helps to solidify them.

Slide 17

→ No collaborative interaction is complete without some thanks and appreciation!

LESSON 34: MIDCOURSE CORRECTIONS

Why Use It?

Midcourse Corrections dramatize how skilled groups constantly and actively monitor their progress . . . the way real "college- and career-ready" people must every day.

Complex, multiday (or multiweek) inquiry projects are often the most memorable experiences kids have in school. But the bigger they are, the more these projects need to be carefully monitored. Sometimes teachers try to ensure organization by creating a lockstep structure and schedule for everyone (purchase white 3 × 5 notecards, and have ten footnotes by Friday).

We much prefer to have students grapple with these decisions for themselves, keeping their own records and finding their own path through self-reflection and negotiation. In that spirit, we have already provided the tools of Project Logs, Work Plans, and Assessment Rubrics. Now, we add a reflection called Midcourse Corrections. These dramatize how skilled groups constantly and actively monitor their progress, both as individuals and as teams: just the way real "college- and career-ready" people must every day.

When to Use It

While this lesson assumes that kids are doing small-group inquiry projects, it can easily be adapted to individual research projects in which kids use each other as sounding boards along the way, but are not co-investigating the same topics.

Preparation

- Tell kids the day before that this lesson is coming, so that they will arrive with all their materials ready to go:
  - Project Logs
  - Individual and Group Work Plans
  - Inquiry Project Calendars
  - Assessment Rubrics

The Lesson

Slide 1

TITLE: **Midcourse Corrections**

Slide 2

→ To keep students on course, we always do this at least once during extended projects, often several times.

Slide 3

→ This is a lot of stuff to manage. Take the time to be sure everyone has these items out and on their desk.

→ Explain that this is something we do periodically once research and work are underway to make sure everyone is on track—and to make adjustments, as needed.

Slide 4

→ A review of the forms as kids dig them out.

Slide 5

→ Have kids copy these questions into their research journals or notebooks, and then jot answers to each.

Slide 6

→ More questions to record and answer.

Slide 7

→ *Now turn to your group, and take turns sharing your individual progress.*

→ *Try to summarize the most important issues.*

→ *Take one minute each.*

→ *Partners, help each other by asking thoughtful follow-up questions.*

→ Time management is the challenge with this step. There is potentially so much that each kid could talk about, so as you circulate, help them be selective as they report out to their groups.

Slide 8

→ Have kids get out their Group Work Plan form to be ready for this step. They will be referring to this as they write and talk.

Slide 9

→ As with the list of *individual* goals, have kids copy these questions into their research journals or notebooks, and then jot answers to each there as well.

Slide 10

→ Once again, kids need to be selective in what they talk and write about. It is fine to coach them actively, even interrupt the group meetings to offer quick suggestions for using the time well.

Slide 11

→ Each group reports out briefly.

→ This is a whole-class gathering and invites students to share some typical progress, problems, and plans.

→ Remind students to:
  ▪ Share the status of their research
  ▪ Share what's next

→ Encourage audience members to ask helpful questions.

→ **Note:** This is a great opportunity to reinforce that ambitious, long-term projects *always* require constant maintenance, refiguring, rescheduling, and the cutting and adding of tasks.

Slide 12

→ A thank you is always in order.

LESSON 35: BEING AN ATTENTIVE AUDIENCE MEMBER

Why Use It?

We want student presentations to be genuine learning opportunities for everyone—and that means everyone must be engaged and thinking.

Projects, individual or group, often culminate in a public presentation or performance. While it's the presenter's duty to be well prepared and entertaining, it's also the audience's responsibility to be attentive and considerate. Defining these expectations explicitly is essential so that no student is sabotaged by behaviors that interfere with his or her concentration. And, above all, we want student presentations to be genuine learning opportunities for everyone—and that means everyone must be engaged and thinking.

When to Use It

Teach this lesson the day before class presentations begin and then refer back to the audience skill chart every time students are performing for their classmates.

Preparation

- Decide ahead of time how partners will pair up.
- Decide how students will record their skill notes.

The Lesson

Slide 1

TITLE: **Being an Attentive Audience Member**

Slide 2

→ Tell students:

- *Surveys still say that people fear public speaking more than anything else except death.*

Slide 3

→ Talk about how we need to support each other:

- *We're each other's team members.*
- *We're each other's fans.*
- *Home Court Advantage is especially relevant, because you are about to become audiences—and fans—for each other.*

Slide 4

→ Project and read aloud.

Slide 5

→ Say something like this:

- *All of you are going to have to get up in front of the room eventually, and the audience can have a big effect on how you perform.*
- *When other people are performing, you are part of the audience. We're all playing on the same team, and we all want everyone to do his or her best. Therefore, we need to talk about what it means to be an attentive audience member.*

Slide 6

→ Demonstrate how to fold and label the paper as students follow along.

Slide 7

→ Read this slide.

→ Emphasize that we will just be examining the *body language* of attentive audience members.

Slide 8

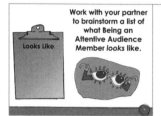

→ Monitor partners as they jot down their body language descriptors. Remind them to focus on positive behaviors.

Slide 9

→ Before the sharing and listing commences, designate a Student Scribe so that you will be free to mingle, monitor, and coach as the class shares.

→ As you call on pairs to contribute to the class master list, be sure to record all the behaviors on the board; or, ideally, briefly switch to projectable word processing. That way, you'll have a permanent copy of the list.

→ If you do write directly on the board, take a photo of the finished Looks Like list with your smartphone before you erase!

→ Instruct students to add new ideas to their Looks Like column so that they have a complete list as well.

→ A typical list will include:

- Interested
- Thoughtful/attentive
- Sitting up straight
- Smiling, nodding
- Enjoying performance
- Caring about what's being said
- Eye contact
- Desk is clear
- Empty hands, except for note taking

Slide 10

→ Now it's time to talk about what attentive audience members sound like.

→ Explain that this is going to be a bit different than the other Sounds Like lists students have made because attentive audience members don't talk during a performance. However, they do make certain appropriate sounds.

Slide 11

→ Have partners flip their papers over to the right-hand column, label it Sounds Like, and begin to brainstorm.

Slide 12

→ Instruct students to add new ideas to their Sounds Like column so that they have a complete list as well.

→ Typical suggestions include:

- Respectful
- No talking
- Applause (appropriate)
- Laughter (appropriate)
- "Crickets"

→ Point out that when you compare the Looks Like list to the Sounds Like list, you'll notice that body language plays a critical role in both. Since an audience's main job during a performance is careful listening, this makes perfect sense.

Slide 13

→ Have students turn back to their partners and briefly talk about how attentive audience behaviors would help them concentrate on their performance.

→ When partners have finished, you might also ask members of the class if they have ever had a moment when someone distracted or "cracked them up" on purpose.

→ *Did this ever happen to anyone when you were doing a presentation or giving a speech?*

→ If some students answer affirmatively, invite them to share their speech story with the rest of the class.

Slide 14

→ If you've evoked some horror stories, make it clear that if an audience member *does* intentionally distract or undermine a performer, that is definitely *not* Home Court behavior.

→ In this room, we are friends, and we support each other.

Slide 15

→ Any collaborative work always ends with thanks!

Resources

LESSON 13: APPOINTMENT CLOCK

LESSON 15: MEMBERSHIP GRID

Name: _____   Date: _____   Hour: _____

Topic and Date	Member Name	Member Name	Member Name	Member Name

LESSON 22: GROUP MEETING PROCEDURES

At the Beginning of a Meeting

☐ Take attendance and determine who will contact missing members in order to bring them up to speed and let them know their responsibilities for the next meeting.

☐ Review Ground Rules.

☐ Determine how the group will incorporate anyone who comes unprepared.

☐ Review Off-Task Trigger Chart.

☐ Review discussion skills that the group plans to use and practice.

☐ Display the table cards.

At the End of a Meeting

☐ Review Ground Rules, discuss how well the group is following them, and determine if any changes need to be made.

☐ Review Off-Task Trigger Chart and discuss how the solutions worked.

☐ Review the group's highlighted discussion skills and discuss how well each was used by members.

☐ Review the day's meeting and make a list of the strengths of today's meeting: What went well? Which parts of the discussion were most interesting/informative/productive?

☐ Review the day's meeting and discuss one or two goals for future meetings that would improve discussion.

☐ Review each member's work completion responsibilities necessary for the next meeting.

☐ Nest the table cards and store for the next meeting.

LESSON 31: THIN-CRUST CHEESE PIZZA RUBRIC

Components	C	B	A
Crust Texture Flavor Color			
Sauce Texture Flavor Color			
Cheese Texture Flavor Color			

LESSON 31: PROJECT RUBRIC

Components	C	B	A

LESSON 32: GROUP WORK PLAN FORM

Names

1.

2.

3.

4.

5.

(Larger groups, please split in two.)

State your **general inquiry topic:**

What are some specific **questions** you plan to pursue? Sometimes it works for groups to divide the main topic into several questions or subtopics for different members to specialize in.

What **research resources** do you expect to use? (Internet, library, interviews, etc.)

(Continued)

(Continued)

What kinds of **help** do you need from your teacher or other adults? Successful inquiry projects require both individual and whole group effort, with tangible outcomes for each. So you need to specify exactly what each member will be doing on their own, **and** how you will work collaboratively to share your learning with others. These plans may change as your research unfolds, so keep me posted and revise your work plan accordingly.

Each person's **individual tangible outcome(s)** should also be listed on the *Individual Group Member Work Plan Forms.*

How will all of us work together to create the group's **culminating event?**

Group Sharing Plan: How are you going to share/perform your new learning for others in the class?

Signatures: We commit to pursue this inquiry as outlined. We will confer with our teacher regularly and make midcourse corrections as needed.

_____   _____

_____   _____

_____   Date: _____

LESSON 32: INDIVIDUAL GROUP MEMBER WORK PLAN FORM

Name:

Date:

Group Topic:

Your subtopic, inquiry question, or specialty:

What **research resources** will you need?

What **help** might you need on your individual work?

What will be your **individual tangible outcome(s)?** (Essay, report, video, podcast, artwork, performance, etc.)

What role will you take in your group's **culminating event?**

I commit to pursue my part of this inquiry project as planned. I will confer with my group and my teacher about any changes in the work or the schedule.

_____ Date: _____

References and Further Readings

Allington, Richard, and Rachael Gabriel. 2012. "Every Child, Every Day." *Educational Leadership.* Vol. 69, No. 6. March.

American Institutes for Research. 2013. *Meaningful Measures: School Discipline That Improves Outcomes.* Washington, DC: American Institutes for Research.

American Psychological Association. 2013. "Teen Suicide Is Preventable." Retrieved from https://www.apa.org/research/action/suicide.aspx

Bradford, Leland. 1978. *Group Development.* San Diego, CA: University Associates.

Breaking Schools Rules: Statewide Study of How School Discipline Relates to Students' Success and Juvenile Justice Involvement. 2011. Retrieved from http://knowledgecenter.csg .org/kc/system/files/Breaking_School_Rules.pdf

Bryk, Anthony, Penny Bender Sebring, Elaine Allensworth, Stuart Luppescu, and John Q. Easton. 2010. *Organizing Schools for Improvement.* Chicago, IL: University of Chicago Press.

Bryk, Anthony, and Barbara Schneider. 2002. *Trust in Schools: A Core Resource for Improvement.* Chicago, IL: Consortium for Chicago Schools Research.

Carter, Carol J. 2013. "How Soft Skills, Passion, and Connection Can Promote Learning, Competence, and Employability." *The Huffington Post.* October 21.

Centers for Disease Control. 2013. "Youth Violence: Facts at a Glance." Retrieved from http://www.cdc.gov/violenceprevention/pdf/yv-datasheet-a.pdf

Cichan, Christine. 2012. "Baltimore City Public Schools' School Discipline Reform Efforts." Retrieved from http://www.fixschooldiscipline.org/toolkit/educators/ baltimore

Committee for Children. 2011. Second Step K–5 Program. Retrieved from http://www .cfchildren.org/Portals/0/SS_K5/K-5_DOC/K-5_Self-Regulation_Skills.pdf

Common Core State Standards for English Language Arts & Literacy in History/Social Studies, Science, and Technical Subjects. 2010. National Governors Association Center for Best Practices and the Council of Chief State School Officers.

Danielson, Charlotte. 2011. *The Framework for Teaching Evaluation Instrument.* Princeton, NJ: The Danielson Group.

Darling-Hammond, Linda, Brigid Barron, P. David Pearson, Alan H. Schoenfeld, Elizabeth K.Stage, Timothy D. Zimmerman, Gina N. Cervetti, and Jennifer L. Tilson. 2008. *Powerful Learning: What We Know About Teaching for Understanding.* San Francisco, CA: Jossey-Bass.

Deutsch, Morton, P. T. Coleman, and E. C. Marcus. 2006. *The Handbook of Conflict Resolution: Theory and Practice,* 2nd edition. San Francisco, CA: Jossey-Bass.

Durlak, Joseph, Roger Weissberg, Allison Dymnicki, Rebecca Taylor, and Kriston Schellinger. 2011. "The Impact of Enhancing Students' Social and Emotional Learning: A Meta-Analysis of School-Based Universal Interventions." *Child Development.* Vol. 82, No.1. January/February, pp. 405–432.

Hanson, Phillip. 1982. *Learning Through Groups.* San Diego, CA: University Associates.

Haynes, Norris M., Michael Ben-Avie, and Jacque Ensign, eds. 2003. *How Social and Emotional Development Add Up: Getting Results in Mathematics and Science Education.* New York: Teachers College Press.

Heitlin, Liana. 2013. "Teachers Use Social-Emotional Programs to Manage Classes." *Education Week.* October 5.

Holland, Sally. 2012. "U.S. Report Finds Inequalities in Courses and Discipline for Minority Students." CNN Online. Retrieved from http://schoolsofthought.blogs

.cnn.com/2012/03/06/u-s-report-finds-inequalities-in-courses-and-discipline-for-minority-students

Jacques, James. 1995. *Learning in Groups.* London: Kogan Page.

Johnson, David, and Roger Johnson. 1987a. *Classroom Conflict.* Edina, MN: Interaction Book Company.

Johnson, David, and Roger Johnson. 1987b. *Learning Together and Alone.* Edina, MN: Interaction Book Company.

Johnson, David, and Roger Johnson. 1989. *Cooperation and Competition: Theory and Research.* Edina, MN: Interaction Book Company.

Johnson, David, and Roger Johnson. 2009. "An Educational Psychology Success Story: Social Interdependence Theory and Cooperative Learning." *Educational Researcher,* Vol. 38, No. 5, pp. 365–379.

Johnson, David, Roger Johnson, and Edythe Holubec. 2008. *Cooperation in the Classroom.* Edina, NM: Interaction Book Company.

Joyce, Bruce, Marsha Weil, and Emily Calhoun. 2003. *Models of Teaching,* 7th edition. Englewood Cliffs, NJ: Prentice Hall.

Kahn, Jennifer. 2013. "Can Emotional Intelligence Be Taught?" *New York Times Magazine.* September 11.

Kapp, Diana. 2013. "Raising Children With an Attitude of Gratitude: Research Finds Real Benefits for Kids Who Say 'Thank You.'" *The Wall Street Journal.* December 23, 2013.

Kluth, Paula, and Alice Udvary-Solner. 2007. *Joyful Learning: Active and Collaborative Learning in Inclusive Classrooms.* Thousand Oaks, CA: Corwin.

Lewin, Kurt. 1948. *Resolving Social Conflicts: Selected Papers on Group Dynamics.* New York: Harper and Brothers.

Lundy, Kathy, and Larry Swartz. 2011. *Creating Caring Classrooms: How to Encourage Students to Communicate, Create, and Be Compassionate of Others.* Portland, ME: Stenhouse.

National Governors Association Center for Best Practices and the Council of Chief State School Officers. 2010. *Common Core State Standards for English Language Arts & Literacy in History/Social Studies, Science, and Technical Subjects.*

Performance Descriptors: Social Emotional Learning. 2003. Illinois State Board of Education.

"Report Tallies Up Inequities in School Discipline Policies. Meaningful Measures: School Discipline That Improves Outcomes." 2013. *Education Week.* November 5.

Schmuck, Richard, and Patricia Schmuck. 2001. *Group Processes in the Classroom.* New York: McGraw-Hill.

Sharan, Schlomo. 1999. *Handbook of Cooperative Learning.* Westport, CT: Greenwood.

Skiba, Russell, Robert S. Michael, Abra Carroll Nardo, and Reece L. Peterson. 2002. "The Color of Discipline: Sources of Racial and Gender Disproportionality in School Punishment." *The Urban Review.* Vol. 34, No. 4. December.

Slavin, Robert. 1994. *Cooperative Learning: Theory, Research, and Practice.* Boston: Allyn and Bacon.

Sparks, Sarah. 2013. "Report Tallies Up Inequities in School Discipline Policies." *Education Week.* Vol. 33, No. 11. November.

Steineke, Nancy. 2002. *Reading and Writing Together: Collaborative Literacy in Action.* Portsmouth, NH: Heinemann.

Texas Essential Knowledge and Skills for English Language Arts and Reading. 2008. Chapter 110. Subchapter C. High School.

Thapa, Armit, Jonathan Cohen, Ann Higgins D'Allessandro, and Shawn Guffey. 2012. *School Climate Research Summary.* New York: National School Climate Center.

Weissberg, Roger P., and Jason Cascarino. 2013. "Academic learning + social-emotional learning = national priority." *Phi Delta Kappan.* October, Vol. 95, No. 2, pp. 8–13.

Yazzie-Mintz, Ethan, Director, High School Survey of Student Engagement. 2009. *Charting the Path From Engagement to Achievement: A Report on the 2009 High School Survey of Student Engagement.* Bloomington: Center for Evaluation & Education Policy, Indiana University.

Zemelman, Steven, Harvey Daniels, and Arthur Hyde. 2012. *Best Practice: Bringing Standards to Life in America's Schools,* 4th edition. Portsmouth, NH: Heinemann.

Index

About the Artist

Satya Moses is a young artist/designer from New Hampshire. He loves writing, doodling, and exploring the wilderness in his homeland of New England. He is also an aspiring world traveler and would like to wander through every continent at some point in his life. This is the first book he has ever illustrated—aside from the ones he put together himself in grade school, which nobody has tried to publish.

CORWIN LITERACY

Harvey "Smokey" Daniels & Elaine Daniels

On that single method for transforming students from passive spectators into active learners

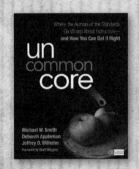

Michael Smith, Deborah Appleman & Jeffrey Wilhelm

On where the authors of the standards go wrong about instruction—and how to get it right

Gretchen Bernabei & Judi Reimer

On 101 lessons and mentor texts for tackling the most persistent issues in academic writing

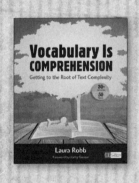

Laura Robb

On helping students tackle the biggest barrier to complex texts

Sara Holbrook & Michael Salinger

On how to teach today's i-touch generation precision writing and reading in any subject

Nancy Boyles

On classroom-ready resources to get close reading right in grades 3–6

To order your copies, visit **www.corwin.com/literacy**

BECAUSE ALL TEACHERS ARE LEADERS

Nancy Frey & Douglas Fisher

On five access points for seriously stretching students' capacity to comprehend complex text

Jim Burke

On what the 6–8 standards really say, really mean, and how to put them into practice

Douglas Fisher & Nancy Frey

On how text-dependent questions can inspire close and critical reading

Jim Burke

On everything you need to know to put the 9–12 standards into practice

Lapp, Wolsey, Wood & Johnson

On using graphic organizers to make the complex comprehensible

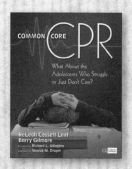

ReLeah Lent & Barry Gilmore

On practical strategies for coaxing our most resistant learners into engagement and achievement

CL CORWIN LITERACY

N14787

CORWIN
A SAGE Company

The Corwin logo—a raven striding across an open book—represents the union of courage and learning. Corwin is committed to improving education for all learners by publishing books and other professional development resources for those serving the field of PreK–12 education. By providing practical, hands-on materials, Corwin continues to carry out the promise of its motto: **"Helping Educators Do Their Work Better."**